Praise for

RETHINKING DRINKING

"This timely and balanced guide bridges rigorous science with real-world practicality. The authors make complex research understandable and usable, whether you want to reexamine your own drinking habits or support a loved one. Unlike many resources on alcohol, this book respects personal choice. I recommend it for its compassionate, nonjudgmental tone and step-by-step guidance."

—Angelo M. DiBello, PhD, Center of Alcohol and Substance Use Studies, Rutgers, The State University of New Jersey

"This is one book where I don't mind spoiling the ending: Drs. Miller and Muñoz wish you all the best in choosing your own way. With more than four decades of research, clinical practice, and authorship between them, they've learned that a simple binary—drink or don't drink—doesn't work for everyone. What we really need is information and guidance that helps us make the best decisions about whether and how we drink. That's where *Rethinking Drinking* comes in. By the time you finish this book, you'll have created an action plan and built the confidence to make your choices a reality."

—Derek Brown, author of *Mindful Mixology*

"Many people today are rethinking their relationship with alcohol, and this book meets that moment well. *Rethinking Drinking* is calm, clear, and grounded. It helps you slow down, take stock, and make choices that fit your life, rather than forcing a single answer about drinking. This is a book you can actually use—not just read."

—Akhil Anand, MD, addiction psychiatrist, Cleveland Clinic

"This book empowers you to make informed choices about drinking that feel right to you. The exploration of the positive things people feel they get out of drinking—and ways to achieve these benefits without alcohol—is unique. I would recommend this book to friends and family members without hesitation."

—Kate B. Carey, PhD, Center for Alcohol and Addiction Studies, Brown University School of Public Health

RETHINKING DRINKING

Also from William R. Miller

FOR GENERAL READERS

8 Ways to Hope: Charting a Path through Uncertain Times
William R. Miller

On Second Thought: How Ambivalence Shapes Your Life
William R. Miller

Quantum Change: When Epiphanies and Sudden Insights Transform Ordinary Lives
William R. Miller and Janet C'de Baca

FOR PROFESSIONALS

Effective Psychotherapists: Clinical Skills That Improve Client Outcomes
William R. Miller and Theresa B. Moyers

Motivational Interviewing, Fourth Edition: Helping People Change and Grow
William R. Miller and Stephen Rollnick

Motivational Interviewing in Diabetes Care
Marc P. Steinberg and William R. Miller

Motivational Interviewing in Health Care, Second Edition: Helping Patients Change Behavior
Stephen Rollnick, William R. Miller, and Christopher C. Butler

Rethinking Substance Abuse: What the Science Shows, and What We Should Do about It
Edited by William R. Miller and Kathleen M. Carroll

Treating Addiction, Second Edition: A Guide for Professionals
William R. Miller, Alyssa A. Forcehimes, and Allen Zweben

RETHINKING DRINKING

Making the Right Choice for You

William R. Miller, PhD
Ricardo F. Muñoz, PhD

THE GUILFORD PRESS
New York London

In grateful memory of Professor Nick Heather
—W. R. M.

To Lily and Avery
—R. F. M.

Printed in the United States of America

For product and safety concerns within the EU, please contact *GPSR@taylorandfrancis.com,* Taylor & Francis Verlag GmbH, Kaufingerstraße 24, 80331 München, Germany.

Last digit is print number: 9 8 7 6 5 4 3 2 1

Library of Congress Cataloging-in-Publication Data

Names: Miller, William R. (William Richard) author | Muñoz, Ricardo F. author
Title: Rethinking drinking : making the right choice for you / William R. Miller, PhD, Ricardo F. Muñoz, PhD.
Description: New York : The Guilford Press, [2026] | Includes bibliographical references and index.
Identifiers: LCCN 2026018847 | ISBN 9781462558704 paperback alk. paper | ISBN 9781462563159 hardcover
Subjects: LCSH: Controlled drinking | Drinking of alcoholic beverages | Alcoholism—Prevention | Self-care, Health
Classification: LCC HV5278 .M553 2026
LC record available at *https://lccn.loc.gov/2026018847*

CONTENTS

Part Four
GETTING WHAT YOU WANT WITHOUT EXPECTING ALCOHOL TO GIVE IT TO YOU

PREFACE

Much attention is being given these days to whether and how much to drink. Both professional journals and the popular press regularly offer articles about the pros and cons of alcohol, as well as how people's use of alcohol has changed over the years. You may be wondering what place drinking should have, if any, in your own life. We believe that people have the right to make decisions about their lifestyles and to have access to accurate information on which to base those choices. We wrote this book to provide a balanced presentation of current knowledge regarding the impact of drinking for individuals and for our communities.

The work on which *Rethinking Drinking* is based actually began more than 50 years ago and has been evolving ever since as new research appears. Our original 1976 volume, *How to Control Your Drinking,* was the first self-help book on moderate alcohol use. A common belief at that time was that there were only two kinds of people in the world: Either you were alcoholic and unable to drink moderately or you were not alcoholic and therefore had no reason for concern because you could drink with impunity. In other words, no one really needed our book.

Nevertheless, people did come to our clinics in Oregon and then New Mexico to learn how to drink moderately. Over a period of 10 years, we completed seven clinical trials to test the effectiveness of this self-control approach. On average, those participating in our studies cut their drinking by half or more, reductions that were well maintained over years of follow-up. We also found that people could successfully use the same methods whether working on their own with this book or with the guidance of a counselor. Other research groups around the world reported similar success with various forms of self-control training.

Over time, 23% of those seeking to learn moderation decided to quit drinking altogether instead. Furthermore, across 7 years of follow-up, if these abstainers did drink on occasion (as most did), it was very little and just for a few days. Then they went back to being nondrinkers.

Another 14% maintained asymptomatic moderation, and a further 22% had substantially reduced their drinking but continued to experience a few problems or signs of dependence.

We soon discovered that we could predict who would drink moderately and who would quit: The more severe their alcohol-related problems and dependence had been, the more likely they were to abstain.

As we discuss in Chapter 1, there have been substantial societal changes as to whether and how people drink. Abstaining from alcohol is common and socially accepted today. Younger generations are not drinking the way their parents and grandparents did. Alcohol is widely recognized as a health risk factor like tobacco, cholesterol, and high blood pressure. Guidelines about what constitutes safe or moderate drinking are changing, and prior reports that a certain amount of drinking is good for you are being questioned.

And still it comes down to choice. What you decide about drinking is up to you. We offer this new book in a very different social context than the one in which we began half a century ago. Part One builds the foundation of knowledge you need to rethink drinking, explaining how drinking has changed in our society (see Chapter 1) and reasons why people drink and don't drink (Chapters 2 and 3). In Part Two we describe what effects alcohol has when one does drink (Chapter 4), then provide you the opportunity to do a personal checkup (Chapter 5) and to consider what, if any, changes you might wish to make (Chapter 6). If you choose to reduce your drinking, Part Three offers some science-tested methods for doing so. Finally, Part Four offers a menu of strategies for satisfying important needs and desires, from relaxing and managing moods to forming and maintaining good relationships, with or without alcohol.

We wish you good health and happiness, whatever you may decide about drinking.

ACKNOWLEDGMENTS

We gratefully acknowledge that countless colleagues, mentors, students, clients, and family have contributed much to our learning over the decades, enabling us to share what follows. The technical production and improvement of this book was greatly aided by the editorial staff at The Guilford Press, particularly Kitty Moore and Chris Benton. What a pleasure it is to work with such helpful and competent professionals who are as committed as their authors to producing a book that is both science-based and readable. Muchas gracias!

* * *

The following material is reprinted or adapted from *Controlling Your Drinking: Tools to Make Moderation Work for You, Second Edition,* by William R. Miller and Ricardo F. Muñoz (copyright © 2013 The Guilford Press; reprinted by permission): Personal Goals Card (page 69), Daily Record Card (page 72), Summary of Progress Form (page 83), and List of Positive Characteristics (page 151).

Part One

GETTING STARTED

1

THE PUZZLE OF ALCOHOL

You may have been noticing some significant social changes regarding alcohol use. In 2025, only 54% of U.S. adults reported that they drink alcohol—the lowest percentage in 90 years of Gallup polling—and for the first time a majority of adults (53%) said that moderate drinking is bad for health.[1] There is Dry January—the challenge to try a month-long break from alcohol after holiday excesses—and, more recently, Sober October. In a popular 2025 family film, *Lilo and Stitch,* extraterrestrials construe a cocktail party to be humans drinking ceremonial poison. You may have noticed too that it's less common for free alcohol to be offered at social events or even in private homes. The public demand for nonalcohol alternatives has grown to the point that it's now common to find "mocktails" on menus, and alcohol-free wines and beers are available in much greater variety and quality.

What accounts for this popularity of alternatives to alcohol? In part it's the surprisingly pleasant results of a Dry January or Sober October experience. What might initially seem like a sacrificial challenge can yield some unexpected benefits: better sleep, sharper thinking and memory, and maybe just plain feeling better. Ruby Warrington's 2019 best-seller *Sober Curious* got people wondering what it might be like to live without alcohol and to try it out, at least for a while.[2] These experiences are not merely for people who drink "too much" or have "an alcohol problem." Ordinary people are starting to wonder about and question the role that alcohol plays in their lives. "Why am I drinking? How important is alcohol to me?" Perhaps that's part of why you're reading this book.

We too have observed a major shift in societal thinking about alcohol. We naturally pay attention because drinking has been a focus of our work for several decades, and choices people make about drinking have been studied for at least half a century. Throughout this time, one of us has been a moderate drinker, the other an abstainer by rational choice, and our own thinking about drinking has been evolving through these years. We've heard stories from so many people about what influenced their own decisions about alcohol and the outcomes of their efforts. Everyone's path is different, and we regard drinking alcohol, like smoking, to be a matter of personal choice.

While social reluctance about drinking has increased, other changes have exacerbated some of the common motivations for using alcohol discussed in Chapter 2. As people spend more time alone with digital media, the U.S. Surgeon General has declared isolation and loneliness to be a health-threatening social epidemic.[3] An ever-widening wealth gap places greater economic stress on many individuals and families.[4,5] The 24/7 news cycle offers ample inducement to seek relief and escape.

We've written this book now to help you reflect on alcohol's role in your life and what you get (or at least hope to get) from drinking. We also offer you some research-tested methods for making any changes that you may choose when you set your own goals.

You are not alone in rethinking drinking. It's been happening all around the world, and, as we describe in this next section, this rethinking has been going on for a long time.

THE EVER-CHANGING FACE OF ALCOHOL

The history of alcohol has been a roller-coaster ride. There were times and places in which most people consumed alcoholic beverages regularly, sometimes as a preferable alternative to water. For many centuries in Judaism and Christianity, wine has held a prominent place in religious rituals. At other times and places, drinking alcohol has been regarded as a moral issue and even a religious taboo. The realization of the toll alcohol can inflict isn't a recent occurrence.

During the late 19th century and up through the 1920s, American public education described alcohol as a dangerous drug that no one could use safely. Within this understanding of alcohol, which had been building up for decades, the 18th Amendment to the U.S. Constitution prohibiting its manufacture, sale, or transportation made sense in 1919. When Prohibition was then repealed just 14 years later, alcohol once again became widely available, and with it an enduring national case of ambivalence: "Yes, we know that alcohol is a dangerous drug, and it's okay." A temporary solution to this mental whiplash quickly emerged in a public and professional consensus that it must be only *certain* people (namely, alcoholics) who were unable to use alcohol safely, whereas the rest of us could drink with impunity.

When we wrote our first book on this subject in 1975, drinking was broadly accepted and often expected as a normal part of social life, even a rite of passage into adulthood. Like smoking, alcohol was regarded as an ordinary, even glamorous, part of life. Characters in movies and TV programs drank and smoked onscreen. In this social environment, those who chose to abstain from alcohol often felt obliged to explain why. Some people even took offense if their friends did not join them in having a drink. Although "drunk" driving was frowned on, in fact drinking before driving was widely accepted as normal. People usually needed cars to reach places serving alcohol (such as bars, restaurants, and sporting events), which were surrounded by large parking lots. Hosts of public or private parties frequently offered a wide range of alcoholic beverages and didn't worry much about how their guests would get home. The three-martini lunch was just a normal part of doing business.

How very much has changed in public and professional views of alcohol! There are now public health guidelines for "safer drinking" (discussed later in this chapter). Years ago, when the risks of lung cancer and other health problems became clear, doctors began asking about their patients' cigarette-smoking habits. Now it's routine to ask about how much alcohol they drink as well. In 2025 the U.S. Surgeon General published a major new advisory report on alcohol and cancers.[6] Since the 1970s the legal intoxication limit for impaired driving has been decreasing worldwide. More recently, awareness of server liability substantially changed how alcohol is offered in both public and private settings. *Sober Curious* launched a social movement of its own, with more people questioning whether they need or want to continue drinking.

What has been your own experience with alcohol since you began drinking? Has your thinking about alcohol shifted in the midst of these social changes? You still see alcohol being used in movies and TV shows, in which the characters tend to drink much more than most people do. Where else do you encounter alcohol? In social gatherings? How about among your friends? Does alcohol ever come up in conversation?

CHANGES IN ALCOHOL USE

As with tobacco smoking, there have already been major changes in U.S. alcohol use, especially among younger adults. Since U.S. alcohol consumption peaked around 1980, it has been gradually declining.[7] Chapter 5 describes current American adult drinking norms so you can compare them with your own alcohol use. When our first book on alcohol was published in 1976, one-third of American adults were nondrinkers, and the remaining two-thirds on average consumed about 4 gallons of pure ethyl alcohol per person per year. That was equal to each drinker having 20 bottles of beer, 20 ounces of distilled spirits, or three bottles of wine per week.[8] The word *average* can be very misleading, however, because most drinkers were actually having less than one drink per day. How can that be? It's because a relatively small percentage of drinkers consume large amounts of alcohol.[9]

TERMS FOR TROUBLE WITH ALCOHOL

The world has also seen changes in the language used to refer to being in trouble with alcohol. Early moralistic names to describe individuals (such as *drunkard*) gave way to diagnostic terms for particular conditions. Medical terminology in general then shifted away from labeling *people* (*diabetics, schizophrenics*) toward describing them as having *illnesses* (*person with diabetes or schizophrenia*). The term *alcoholism* has not been a formal diagnosis since 1980, when it was replaced by *alcohol abuse* and *alcohol dependence*,[10] but the term *abuse* still had obvious pejorative overtones, implying that people were somehow mistreating alcohol itself. One wry colleague quipped that an example of "abusing" alcohol is mixing a single-malt scotch with root beer. It also became clear that so-called abuse and dependence were not really distinct conditions, and so now *alcohol use disorders* are recognized as varying along a range of severity.[11]

One way to describe trouble with alcohol is *overdrinking,* just as *overeating* or *overworking* mean overdoing it. Overdrinking implies exceeding a limit, raising the much-discussed issue of how much is too much. We suggest three different ways to think about *too much:* risky, harmful, and dependent drinking.

Risky Drinking

Risky drinking means alcohol is already putting you or others in danger, although it may not have caused obvious harm so far.

Risky drinking is measured using three factors. The first is the *overall amount* of alcohol you consume. For example, what dose of alcohol over time makes a negative consequence such as cancer more likely to occur? "Low-risk" drinking is often defined in this way—as a level of alcohol consumption with lower likelihood of causing harm. "Low risk," of course, requires a judgment about how much risk is acceptable.

The second factor is how much alcohol you have *at one time.* Even a single occasion of drinking can have harmful consequences. An obvious example is a fatal overdose of alcohol. A large dose of alcohol can also trigger health dangers such as low blood sugar or irregular heartbeat. In Chapter 4 we discuss in more detail the effects of particular levels of alcohol in the body.

The third factor is the *situations* in which you drink. Risky drinking by this measure means using alcohol in particular circumstances in which even a single occasion can have tragic consequences. A clear example is drinking and driving. Laws usually define unacceptable risk at a particular blood alcohol concentration (BAC) level. Since 2004 it has been illegal in all 50 states to operate a motor vehicle at a BAC of .08 (grams of alcohol per 100 milliliters of blood, abbreviated as mg%). Like Canada, Utah has already lowered that limit to .05, which further reduces fatal crashes,[12] and in most of Mexico the limit is .05 or .04. However, important driving functions such as reaction time, vigilance, alertness, and divided attention are already being impaired at even lower BAC levels.[13] For California drivers who are under 21 years of age or on probation for driving under the influence, the BAC limit is .01. The only truly safe level of alcohol in your bloodstream when driving is *zero.* The same is true when engaged in critical occupations such as performing surgery or piloting aircraft. Other obvious examples of risky situations include drinking when swimming or using machinery such as a chainsaw. Drowning and life-threatening accidents are far more likely to happen when alcohol is present in the body.

So how many adults are risky drinkers at present? As we discuss in Chapter 5, about 1 in 11 adults *regularly* drink more than the currently recommended dietary amounts. But even more people are risky drinkers by virtue of how much they occasionally drink. Perhaps the best measure of this is self-reported binge drinking within the preceding month, commonly defined as five or more standard drinks on one occasion for a man, four or more standard drinks for a woman. That has been about one in six U.S. adults.[14] There is also overlap among these kinds of risky drinking. Some but not all people who regularly exceed dietary recommendations also drink too much on occasion or in unwise situations.

Harmful Drinking

For about 1 in 20 adults, their current drinking is not just risky but has already been causing harm to themselves or others within the previous year.[15] Former terms for this were *problem drinking*[16] or *alcohol abuse.*[17] Alcohol can contribute to many kinds of harm, including physical or mental illness, dementia, impaired performance at school or work, family conflict, violent crime, economic or legal trouble, injuries, and disability. In the course of a lifetime, about one in five U.S. adults have experienced harm from their own alcohol use and still more from others' drinking.[15]

Dependent Drinking

Finally, drinking can progress to the point at which it is not only harmful but also the person becomes *dependent* on alcohol, finding it difficult to feel normal and live without it. People who have become dependent on alcohol may have to drink more to feel the effect they want, and, when that effect wears off, they may experience discomfort that, like a hangover, is relieved by more alcohol. They begin to avoid previously enjoyed activities, spend more time drinking and recovering, have trouble quitting or cutting down, and keep drinking in spite of adverse consequences. Over the course of a lifetime, alcohol dependence happens to one in eight American adults, and in any 1 year it's nearly 4%, or about 10 million U.S. adults.[15]

Although those with alcohol dependence are more noticeable and more likely to receive treatment, in fact it is the nondependent risky and harmful drinkers who account for most of the adverse consequences of alcohol use discussed in Chapter 3, because they are far more numerous than the dependent drinkers.

One international effort to prevent these detrimental effects of alcohol has been to recommend lower risk levels of drinking.[18,19] We need to point out here that "lower risk drinking" is not necessarily *safe* drinking. In our 2013 book, *Controlling Your Drinking,* we said: "At relatively low levels of use, alcohol has no harmful effects for most people and may even offer some health benefits." In light of more recent research, we now must question that statement. The World Health Organization recently stated that there may not be a truly safe level of drinking.[20] Even low levels of alcohol consumption, for example, can increase risk for several types of cancer.[6] Recent studies have also questioned earlier reports that low levels of alcohol use may offer health benefits. In Chapters 4 and 5, we consider these issues in more detail.

HOW TO USE THIS BOOK

The journey of rethinking drinking continues in the chapters ahead. In Chapter 2, we discuss reasons that people in general drink—what positive things they experience or at least hope to get by using alcohol.

Then, in Chapter 3, we examine the other side of the balance, common reasons for not drinking or cutting down. How important these pros and cons are *to you* is a personal matter. You can weigh them on your own scales.

The chapters ahead are for better understanding and rethinking your personal use of alcohol. In Chapters 2 and 3 you can consider your own reasons for using and not using alcohol. Then in Part Two you can learn more about alcohol's effects (Chapter 4) and do a private checkup of your drinking (Chapter 5) before putting it all together in considering where to go from here (Chapter 6).

In Part Three we offer a variety of research-tested steps for reducing your drinking if that's what you choose to do. We've been developing and testing these self-control strategies for five decades and have results from seven clinical trials on how well they work and for whom.

Finally, whatever you decide to do, it's useful to have things you can do to get what you want from life without expecting alcohol to provide it, and that's the subject of Part Four. If alcohol happens to be the main or only way you have for seeking what many of us want, you can explore some new roads for getting to where you want to be. Then you are free to choose.

2

REASONS FOR DRINKING

Why do you drink alcohol? Why does anybody drink?

SIX BIG REASONS FOR DRINKING

When asked this question, people give dozens of different answers that tend to fall into clusters of reasons that we call the Big Six. Here they are.

1. For Enjoyment

One set of reasons to drink has to do with sheer enjoyment. You may simply like the taste or enjoy the feeling that comes when you have a drink or two. Sometimes it's to have fun or celebrate on a special occasion. A drink can symbolize a pleasant transition from work to play, like at the end of a hard day or week. Perhaps you appreciate discerning subtleties of taste and fancy yourself a good judge of wines, beers, or scotch: "I just like it."

2. For Relationships

A second set of reasons for drinking is linked with other people. Some drink to fit in, to be polite or part of the group. It could be that people who are drinkers expect you to drink, too. You want to belong, and it might seem strange to them if you didn't have a drink. Or maybe you drink with one particular person and alcohol is important in that relationship.

3. To Socialize

Some people drink because it helps them relax and feel less shy, more outgoing, at ease, and confident. It seems to be harder to have a good time and let go around other people without alcohol as a lubricant. Sometimes drinking seems to help sex happen or be better.

4. For Relief

Other motivations for using alcohol are about making an unpleasant experience go away, at least temporarily. It might be for relief from sadness, boredom, irritation, guilt, disturbing memories, or just feeling bad about yourself.

5. To Be Drunk

Some people tell us that "I drink to get drunk." They enjoy the effects of more than a few drinks, and it's a break from being sober. "Having a drink or two just isn't the same. It doesn't do it for me."

6. Necessity

Then there are times when alcohol seems necessary. The feeling is that you *must* have a drink, that you can't *not* drink. It might be to concentrate or feel normal, to relieve a hangover, or to stave off alcohol withdrawal.

What do you think? To what extent is each of these a reason you use alcohol? How important would you say each one is in your own drinking? Take a moment now to assign each of the six reasons a letter rating for its importance and write it down below or on a separate note. You're going to need it for your personal checkup if you read Chapter 5.

A	Definitely! That's important for me.
B	Mostly that's true for me.
C	That matters a little—it's somewhat true for me.
D	Not at all. That's definitely not a reason why I drink.

______	______	______	______	______	______
Enjoyment	Relationships	Socializing	Relief	Being drunk	Necessity

Now, you may have additional reasons for drinking that don't seem to fall into any of these categories. That's okay. These are just the most common ones. We also know that sometimes the categories can overlap a bit, as with Relationships and Socializing. Priests might say that drinking some wine is a necessary part of their job. What matters here is for you to take a close, honest look at the reasons *you* drink, just for your own private consideration.

HEALTH BENEFITS OF DRINKING

One potential reason for drinking that is not included in the Big Six is for health benefits. Although heavy drinking is clearly harmful, some people have believed that moderate alcohol use is good for you. In a recent Gallup poll, 6% of American adults said that drinking one or two drinks a day is good for your health, 53% believed it's bad for your health, and 37% thought it makes no difference.[1] In Jewish and

Christian scripture, there is no blanket disapproval of alcohol, although intoxication and harmful drinking are consistently condemned.[2] One Psalm sings that wine "gladdens the heart," and the apostle Paul advised Timothy to stop drinking only water and "take a little wine for the sake of your stomach and your frequent ailments."[3] Does moderate alcohol use actually bestow health benefits that are not enjoyed by those who abstain?

The idea that drinking alcohol can make you healthier is now being seriously questioned by research. It is true that in general population studies moderate drinkers are usually found to have lower rates of heart disease and death when compared with total abstainers. The problem is that there are many possible reasons for such differences besides a beneficial effect of drinking a little alcohol. Nondrinkers are different from moderate drinkers in many ways besides their use of alcohol. Abstainers include former drinkers who are in recovery from past alcohol problems. Some are nondrinkers by moral or religious belief; others for legal reasons such as probation and parole, or medical reasons such as illness, medication use, diabetes, or pregnancy. In a study of 30 risk factors for cardiovascular disease and mortality, nondrinkers were found to be higher than moderate drinkers on 27 of them.[4] After adjusting for these risk factors, it appears that whatever health advantage light drinkers may have compared to abstainers is probably not caused by alcohol itself.[5] We acknowledge that researchers still disagree about purported health benefits of moderate drinking.[6] Having reviewed this large and growing literature ourselves, we believe that a benevolent effect of moderate alcohol use on health seems doubtful. Certainly alcohol is not the only or most effective way to reduce your risk of heart disease and premature death.

The act of having a drink can produce effects that have nothing to do with the alcohol (see Chapter 4), that is, placebo effects. If you believe that alcohol is going to reduce your stress or anxiety and help you relax, then it may happen. Placebo effects are well known in both pharmacological and psychological research, such as in relieving pain. Again, alcohol is not the only or most effective way to reduce stress and anxiety. Part Four of this book is all about other ways to respond to the challenges of life and to reach goals that many of us share.

Deciding whether to do something involves weighing the pros and cons, the potential benefits as well as costs and risks.[7,8] That's true in deciding whether to exercise, travel, make an investment, have a health checkup, or change jobs. Comparing the pros and cons also applies to using substances such as tobacco or alcohol. People have various reasons for drinking, as discussed in this chapter. Next we consider potential reasons for not drinking.

3

REASONS FOR NOT DRINKING

There was a time when people who abstained from alcohol felt obliged to explain why they weren't drinking. These days, however, most of us know that many people don't drink, and this question can seem as inappropriate as asking someone "Why don't you climb trees?"

Just as there are various motivations for using alcohol (Chapter 2), there are also many different reasons that people have for not drinking, even on a particular occasion. Lifelong abstainers most often say that they just have no interest in drinking.[1] Some grew up in nondrinking families or cultures, and "It's just how I was brought up." Those who have a family history or lived experience of alcoholism may choose to avoid the risk themselves.

Other people have religious or moral reasons to refrain from using alcohol. Jewish, Christian, and Islamic scriptures recognize alcohol as a part of life and also warn of its dangers. Some large religions prohibit or at least strongly discourage alcohol use. Individuals may choose on moral grounds not to support alcohol and tobacco industries or to refrain from drinking in solidarity with those who make this choice.

Others are part of a nondrinking culture: "Most of my friends don't drink."

Among former drinkers who now abstain, many say they have no interest in drinking, and they often cite health concerns.[2] Others had serious alcohol-related problems from which they are now recovering.[3] Even current drinkers sometimes refrain from alcohol or reduce their drinking on certain occasions out of concerns such as safety, social disapproval, weight gain, or cost.[4,5]

THE WRATH OF GRAPES

Concerns about the effects of alcohol on health, safety, and well-being are warranted. Undeniably, drinking a lot is bad for you. The term *alcoholism* was first used by the Swedish physician Magnus Huss in 1849 to describe the effects of drinking that he saw in his patients.[6] His explanation of alcohol's effects on the body was straightforwardly simple: Alcohol is a toxin, a poison. The progressive effects of intoxication parallel those of poisoning from other toxic substances—blurring of cognition, vomiting, impaired walking and balance, sedation, unconsciousness, and, at high doses, death. Huss also described chronic toxic effects of drinking, such as "slow alcohol poisoning of the brain," which is now well documented. He further noted that drinkers have elevated rates of accidents and violence, including sexual assault and suicide, sometimes occurring during a single tragic incident of intoxication. He could have been writing in the 21st century.

It's clear that the more you drink, the greater the risk you run for a whole range of health problems.[7] The liver is affected directly because it's the main organ responsible for metabolizing alcohol, which is the most common cause of liver disease worldwide, ranging from fatty liver to hepatitis and cirrhosis.[8,9] An individual's level of alcohol consumption is related to their risk for high blood pressure, stroke, coronary artery disease, and heart attack.[7] It has long been known that some of the earliest damaging effects of alcohol are observable in the central nervous system. Heavy drinking can cause enduring impairment of cognitive functions that resembles premature aging, as well as physical shrinkage of the brain, effects that are partially reversible with abstinence.[10–12] Adolescents and older adults may be particularly vulnerable to alcohol-related brain damage.[10,13]

Alcohol use is a major cause of premature deaths. Annually an estimated 178,000 U.S. adults (488 per day) die from preventable causes that are completely attributable to alcohol, such as ethanol poisoning, alcohol cardiomyopathy, alcohol-induced pancreatitis and liver disease, and fetal alcohol exposure.[14] Alcohol-related causes account for about 1 in 10 deaths among working-age adults and an average of 29 years of potential life lost.[15]

Recent research indicates that health risks related to alcohol begin at surprisingly low levels of consumption. A large 2025 study concluded that 1 in 1,000 people who consume more than seven standard drinks per week will die from alcohol-related causes, a risk that increases to 1 in 100 for those who have more than nine drinks per week.[16] A 2025 report from the U.S. Surgeon General[17] warned that alcohol use is a leading cause of at least seven kinds of cancer throughout the gastrointestinal system and of breast cancer in women: "The more alcohol consumed, the greater the risk of cancer . . . this risk may start to increase around one or fewer drinks per day" (page 3). In addition to cancers of the gastrointestinal tract, even moderate drinking contributes to gastritis and acid reflux, with risk for pancreatitis increasing with heavier drinking.[18–21] A summary of research from 195 nations concluded that the only level of alcohol use that minimizes health risk is zero.[22] In other words, again, there is no completely safe level of drinking.

Beyond the overall long-term impact of drinking on the body, alcohol has some more immediate effects. It certainly affects sleep, which is important in maintaining your health. Some people drink to help them get to sleep, and a dose of alcohol does tend to shorten the time needed to fall asleep.[23] Unfortunately, it also disrupts the later quality of sleep by exacerbating restlessness, early waking, and breathing problems.[24,25] Drinking can also contribute to weight gain because ethyl alcohol contains calories without nutrient value. One standard drink of beer or liquor adds about 150 calories; a bit less (125) for a standard drink of wine, 100 of which are from the ethanol itself. Thus drinking alcoholic beverages can cause weight gain, particularly among heavier drinkers.[26,27] The use of alcohol, which is a depressant drug, can also contribute to and exacerbate depression.[28,29]

As Huss observed, alcohol is also tied to violence, particularly among young people, with men often being the victims in bars and women more likely to suffer violence at home.[30] Alcohol in the body increases the likelihood of being either a perpetrator or a victim of aggression and violence.[31] Alcohol use by offender and/or victim precedes about half of all sexual assaults.[32,33] Nations with higher levels of alcohol use per person have higher rates of suicide, and those persons who successfully complete suicide often have elevated rates of alcohol on autopsy.[34,35]

At the end of Chapter 2 we asked you about your reasons for drinking and how important each one is to you. Now here is a list of possible motivations to drink less (or not at all). How important is each of these reasons for you personally? Choose one of these letter ratings for each reason listed in the box on the facing page.

A This is a ***very*** important reason for me to drink less.
B This matters to me as a reason to drink less.
C This is a minor reason for me to drink less.
D No, this is not at all a reason for me to drink less.

There is also space at the bottom for you to add other reasons that matter to you.

Some Reasons to Drink Less Alcohol	
	How important?
To sleep better	
To lose weight	
To avoid supporting the alcohol industry	
To have more money to spend for other things	
To protect my health	
To stay out of trouble	
To be more alert and aware	
To improve my mental health	
To be an example for others	
In solidarity with people who don't drink	
For moral or religious reasons	
Other reason:	
Other reason:	

Part Two

UNDERSTANDING YOUR DRINKING

4

THE EFFECTS OF ALCOHOL WHEN DRINKING

To understand any drug, it's important to know how it affects the body. This chapter is about just that: changes that occur in your body and behavior when drinking ethyl alcohol.

You might guess how much alcohol somebody has consumed from how they look and behave. Actors and comedians portray intoxication through compromised balance, staggering, and slurred speech. However, people with high alcohol tolerance may look sober when they are not (more on this later in this chapter). Perhaps you gauge your own level of inebriation from how you feel, but relying on subjective feelings and impressions has serious limitations. It can be difficult to know at a particular moment just how affected you or someone else is by alcohol.

Medical and law enforcement professionals use a more reliable measure: the amount of alcohol that is circulating in the bloodstream. This is usually expressed as a decimal: the number of grams of ethanol per deciliter of blood. Blood alcohol content (BAC) is most accurately determined from a blood sample but can also be closely estimated from a breath test as alcohol evaporates through the lungs. BAC can vary upward from .00 (no alcohol present) to very high levels over .40.

It's no mystery how alcohol gets in. After being swallowed, it is absorbed through the lining of the stomach and gastrointestinal tract directly into the bloodstream; then it circulates throughout the body until it can be removed. A little is eliminated through breath, sweat, and urine, but about 90% of alcohol has to be broken down by your liver. When you have food in your stomach, it can take longer for alcohol to be absorbed into the bloodstream, but once it's in the blood there's nothing you can do to speed up its elimination. It just takes time, and, as with other drugs, alcohol's effects on the body and behavior depend on the dose.

The box on page 27 shows you some typical effects of various BAC levels. Notice, for example, that impairment of judgment is observable around a BAC of .06, and vomiting normally happens at a BAC near .12. A memory *blackout*—having little or no recall for what happened—typically occurs above a BAC of .20. Adult drinkers usually lose consciousness around .30, and the average fatal dose for adults is .45.

The main thing that determines your BAC is how much alcohol you consume and how long you take to drink it. Drinking on an empty stomach causes your BAC to rise faster because the alcohol is absorbed more quickly into your bloodstream. When you've eaten food before drinking, the alcohol doesn't get through quite as rapidly, but your body still has to eliminate all the ethanol. The main control that you have over your BAC is how much and how quickly you drink.

BAC is also influenced by other factors that you can't control. Even when drinking the same amount of alcohol, women reach a higher BAC than men do; they are more intoxicated. There are several reasons for this. Some have to do with the distribution of muscle and fat cells. Men also break down ethanol in the stomach more quickly than women do. Furthermore, women tend to be smaller, and body weight influences BAC. If drinking the same quantity of ethanol, a person weighing 160 pounds will reach a much higher BAC than someone who weighs 240 pounds.

Typical Effects of BAC Levels

BAC	Effects
.02	Light and moderate drinkers may begin to notice some subtle effects. This is the approximate BAC after one drink.
.04	Most light and moderate drinkers begin to feel relaxed. At this level there is enough impairment of reaction time, alertness, and fine motor skills that driving can be affected. The only truly "safe" BAC when driving is zero.
.06	Judgment, perception, learning, memory, coordination, sexual arousal, attention, and self-control begin to be impaired. Without necessarily being aware of it, you are less likely to make rational decisions about capabilities (to drive, swim, etc.) and are more likely to take risks you would not take if sober. Of course, it's hard to judge when your judgment has been clouded.
.08	Definite impairment of muscle coordination and driving skills. Driving at this BAC level is illegal in all 50 states.
.10	Clear deterioration in memory, reaction time, control and coordination of movements.
.12	Vomiting typically occurs around this level unless it is reached slowly or there is substantial tolerance to alcohol. Vomiting is the body's first line of defense against overdose.
.15	Balance is impaired.
.20	Many people experience a "blackout" and will have no memory of all or part of what happened while BAC was above this level. For youth this can be a fatal dose.
.30	Most people lose consciousness—the body's last protection against overdose.
.45	The average fatal dose for adults; breathing and heartbeat stop.

There are some inherited differences in alcohol metabolism. When ethanol is broken down by the liver, the first byproduct is *acetaldehyde,* and it's highly toxic, even more than ethanol itself. It's not a chemical that you want hanging around in your body for very long. As acetaldehyde builds up, blood pressure increases; you get flushed in the face, may have headaches and stomachaches, might vomit, and generally feel bad. If that sounds like a bad hangover, it is. Fortunately, there are natural enzymes that break down acetaldehyde. Women are slower in metabolizing acetaldehyde, and so are some Asian populations. If you get red in the face when drinking alcohol, you may be piling up acetaldehyde.

In Chapter 5 we offer you information to help you estimate what BAC you are likely to reach based on your weight, gender, and the amount of alcohol you consume. If you're healthy, BAC typically drops by about .015 per hour on average, so it would take about 10 hours to metabolize a BAC of .150.

ALCOHOL TOLERANCE

As with other drugs, there are individual differences in how people respond to ethanol. You may know people who can really "hold their liquor" and can drink others "under the table." Even when matched pound for pound and drink for drink, they will still be awake and reasonably vertical when others have passed out. To some extent, alcohol tolerance is hereditary, but it also is developed by practice, practice, practice. The more you drink, the more your body adapts to the presence of alcohol.

For some, this is a cause for bragging rights: "Alcohol doesn't affect me as much!" But the truth is that alcohol tolerance is bad news. It does not mean that the BAC is low or that the person is unimpaired. A body with alcohol tolerance is like a house without a smoke alarm; there is no built-in warning system that you're in trouble. Even without your feeling or showing it, the alcohol is still there and doing damage. Rather than being admirable, alcohol tolerance is reason for concern. In fact, it's one of the main risk factors for developing alcohol dependence, as well as adverse medical and social consequences of drinking.

We mentioned that the average fatal dose of ethanol is .45, but your local police department may have a list of members of "the 600 Club," people arrested while driving with a BAC of .60 or higher. Not driving *well,* mind you, but nevertheless awake and operating a motor vehicle. The human body has an amazing ability to adapt to adversity, and in this case it's no blessing for them or others.

Is It Drinking or Thinking?

A *placebo* is a pill or other treatment that contains no active ingredients and therefore would be expected to have no beneficial effect. Yet placebo effects are well known in medicine, the psychological result of *believing* that you have received a potentially effective treatment. Although there is nothing of value in the pill itself, people who are given placebo treatment often experience substantial pain relief and reduction of symptoms. If a person is warned about possible "side effects" of the placebo, these often appear. Placebo effects are so substantial that, when new medications are tested, being better than nothing isn't good enough. A new drug has to be more effective than a placebo in clinical trials in which patients are randomly assigned to receive either the actual medication or an identical-looking placebo. Neither medical staff nor the patients themselves know who is receiving the "real" treatment or placebo, and improvement often occurs in both groups. In other words, some "effects" of taking a drug are not due to the drug itself.

Alcohol is no exception. When given drinks that they think contain alcohol, people experience signs of intoxication; they drink and want more of the beverage and begin to feel happier, more relaxed and disinhibited, more talkative and sociable.[1,2] Even when there is no alcohol in the drinks, there is activation in parts of the brain associated with the experience of pleasure.[3] Up to 89% of people who are given such placebo drinks report some experiences of intoxication.[4] Thus some of the joy of drinking is not from alcohol. Just like placebo pain relief, the effects are real but are not caused by ethanol.

Consider the experience of "happy hour." The work or stresses of the day are over. You move to a pleasant environment, maybe with music and friends or someplace quiet and peaceful. You have a drink or two and immediately begin to feel better. Your mood improves, and you start to relax. Is it because of the alcohol?

The diagram below illustrates what has been called the *biphasic effect of drinking*.[5,6] How the same depressant drug can improve mood at a low dose and then steadily worsen it at a higher dose has been a puzzle. One way to understand this phenomenon is that the experiences at a "low dose" may be social and psychological placebo effects

THE "BIPHASIC" EFFECT OF DRINKING

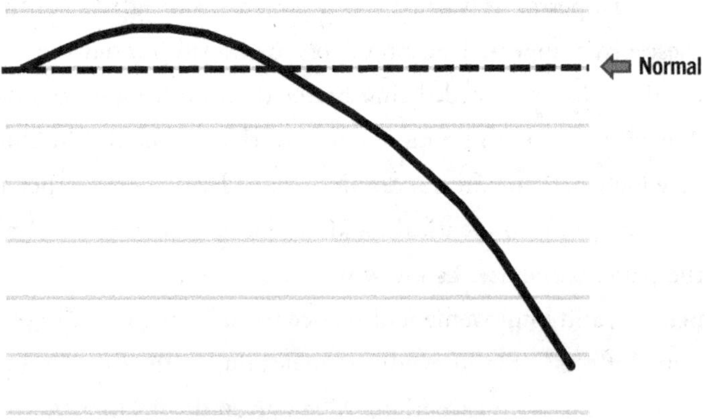

that are eventually overcome by the actual chemical effects of alcohol. Drinkers may literally have a happy *hour.*

Another puzzle is that if you ask people on the next day how they felt while they were drinking, they often remember feeling better—happier and more relaxed. However, if you interview people about how they feel *while* they are drinking at higher BAC levels, they usually report feeling bad, or at least the initially positive mood effects are gone. What's that about? Remember that the accuracy of memory is already degrading around a BAC of .06 and is clearly impaired by .10. So it is easier to recall the earlier positive experiences, whereas later negative effects of drinking are harder to remember. Above .20 there may be no memory at all. Whatever "buzz" or pleasure comes with drinking is likely to happen early, and more alcohol just tends to reverse it.

The actual chemical effects of ethanol happen whether or not you recognize and remember them. You may not realize it, but as BAC increases, deterioration does occur in judgment, reaction time, attention, memory, learning, and coordination. Alcohol tolerance offers no protection against this; it just allows you to endure and ignore higher BAC levels while they do their damage.

IMMEDIATE VERSUS LONG-TERM EFFECTS

What we've been discussing in this chapter is the *immediate* effects of a dose of ethyl alcohol on a particular drinking occasion. These acute effects can be dangerous in themselves, for example, when engaged in risky behavior such as driving with alcohol in your bloodstream. The effects of individual doses of ethanol can also accumulate over time.

Chapter 5 puts together these facts about immediate and long-term effects of alcohol in a self-guided personal checkup. Then Chapter 6 provides an opportunity for you to set goals for yourself and consider possible next steps toward them.

5

A PERSONAL CHECKUP

Now we offer you an opportunity to take what you've learned so far and use it to do a little personal reflection about your alcohol use. This chapter is based on a "drinker's checkup" model that was developed at the University of New Mexico,[1,2] tested in a large nationwide clinical trial,[3,4] computerized for self-administration,[5,6] and later adapted for self-evaluation of marijuana use.[7] The do-it-yourself version in this chapter has just six sections. We were able to offer much more with in-person checkups, such as a blood sample for liver function and some cognitive testing for earlier effects of alcohol on the brain. Computer-administered alcohol checkups are commercially available at *https://checkupandchoices.com* and *https://echeckuptogo.com/programs/alcohol.*

The information in this chapter is just for your own honest consideration. What you do with the information you learn is up to you.

STEP 1. ALCOHOL USE

A first step is to consider the *amount* you drink, just as some people keep track of calories or carbohydrates in what they eat. All types of alcoholic beverages—whether beer, wine, or distilled spirits—contain the same kind of alcohol: ethanol. This makes it possible to calculate how much alcohol you consume, just like counting calories. To do the math, you just multiply the number of ounces of a beverage by the percentage of alcohol it contains.

12 oz. of beer at 5% ethanol: 12 × .05 = 0.6 oz. alcohol

5 oz. of wine at 12% ethanol: 5 × .12 = 0.6 oz. alcohol

1.50 oz. of 80-proof liquor: 1.50 × .40 = 0.6 oz. alcohol

Notice that all of these drinks contain the exact same amount of ethanol, which is called one *standard drink.* For distilled spirits, the *proof* of liquor is just double its percentage of alcohol, so 86 proof = 43% ethanol. The same calculation works with larger amounts of beverage:

Six pack of beer = 6 × 12 = 72 oz. × .05 = 3.6 oz. of alcohol or 6 standard drinks

Bottle of wine = 25.4 oz. × .12 = 3 oz. of alcohol or 5 standard drinks

8 ounces of 86-proof liquor = 8 × .43 = 3.44 oz. of alcohol or 5.7 standard drinks

But math isn't required for this checkup. All you need to do is count up the number of standard drink units in the beverages you prefer, remembering that one standard drink is 12 oz. of beer, 5 oz. of wine, or 1½ oz. of 80-proof liquor.

Now, if your alcohol use is fairly consistent, think about a typical week. What do you normally have to drink on each day of that week? Then add up your number of standard drinks per week. If your drinking is more variable, take a blank calendar page, write in what you might drink on each day in the course of 4 or 5 weeks, then figure out an average week (which does require a little division). What you're looking for is an honest estimate of how many standard drink units you have per week.

Once you have your number, you can compare it with the table on the facing page to find out what percentage of American men or women drink at least that much alcohol. The data in the table come from a carefully conducted national survey that is completed every 5 years using standardized scientific methods.

A few things in this drinking norms table may surprise you. First, more than half of all adults (58%) have one drink a week or less. This includes people who don't drink alcohol at all (25% of men and 31% of women), as well as occasional drinkers who have a drink now and then. If you associate mostly with people who drink regularly, you may wonder, "Who are all those people?" With increasing awareness of related health concerns, overall alcohol use has been declining gradually since the 1980s. Fewer people are drinking, and those who do are drinking less. Only 23% of men and 13% of women have as much as one drink per day. Only 1 in 10 adults have two or more drinks a day (12% of men, 7% of women).

During in-person checkups, people were able to ask questions and discuss their individual results. When encountering surprising information, they have sometimes said things like this:

"I guess I've never really added it up before."

"That can't be right. There must be something wrong with the data."

"Were people being honest on that survey?"

"It says only 6% of people drink as much I do, but everybody I know drinks that much, and some of them more!"

As a reader, you're on your own in making sense of this. You can double-check your work. What we can tell you is that the table contains

U.S. Adult Drinking Norms

DRINKS PER WEEK	HOW MANY U.S. ADULTS DRINK THAT MUCH (OR MORE)?		
	MEN	WOMEN	TOTAL
1	50%	35%	42%
2	39%	26%	33%
3	35%	22%	28%
4	31%	19%	25%
5	28%	16%	22%
6	25%	15%	20%
7	23%	13%	18%
8	20%	12%	16%
9	18%	11%	14%
10	17%	10%	13%
11	15%	9%	12%
12	14%	8%	11%
13	13%	8%	11%
14	12%	7%	10%
15	12%	6%	9%
16–17	11%	6%	8%
18–19	9%	5%	7%
20–21	8%	4%	6%
22–23	8%	3%	6%
24–26	7%	3%	5%
27–30	6%	3%	4%
31–36	5%	2%	4%
37–42	4%	2%	3%
43–49	3%	1%	2%
50–59	3%	1%	2%
60–69	2%	1%	1%
70+	1%	<1%	1%

Source: 2020 National Alcohol Survey of 9,668 individuals. Alcohol Research Group, 6001 Shellmound Street, Suite 450, Emeryville, California 94608, *www.arg.org.*

Courtesy of Drs. Thomas K. Greenfield, *tgreenfield@arg.org*, and Priscilla Martinez, *pmartinez@arg.org*, National Alcohol Survey, NIAAA-supported Alcohol Research Center Grant (P50AA005595; PI William C. Kerr, PhD); with thanks to biostatistician Yu Ye, *yye@arg.org*.

some of the most accurate survey data available. The federally funded National Alcohol Surveys have been performed for five decades by highly experienced research teams.

STEP 2. RISKY DRINKING

A second step in your personal checkup has to do with unwise or risky drinking: using alcohol in a way that places you or others in danger of harm. The implicit question here is, "How much is too much?" As mentioned in Chapter 1, there are three different and overlapping kinds of risky drinking.

One type of risk comes from the overall amount you drink. In Step 1 you estimated the number of standard drinks you consume in a typical week and then compared it with adult norms. Of course, your own health is not directly affected by how much other people drink, but just by your own use of alcohol. There is extensive research on how drinking affects people's health, at least in the long run. Some nations publish recommendations for lower risk drinking. For years the U.S. recommendation has been for men to have no more than two standard drinks per day and for women to have no more than one per day. However, there is no level of consumption at which alcohol use suddenly becomes risky; said another way, there is no amount of drinking with zero health risk. The World Health Organization cautions that "Alcohol consumption, even at low levels can bring health risks."[8] As of 2023,[9] Canada's guidance on alcohol and health is that nondrinking has health benefits, but one to two standard drinks per week "will likely avoid alcohol-related consequences," whereas having three to six drinks per week increases your risk for several types of cancer, as we discussed in Chapter 3. "High risk" is seven or more standard drinks per week.[9]

A second kind of risk has to do with drinking too much at one time. As discussed in Chapter 4, an average fatal dose of alcohol for adults is around .45, although much lower levels may be lethal for children and young adults. This is more common than you might guess. Just among U.S. veterans, 2,421 died from alcohol-involved overdose during the period 2012–2018, 868 from alcohol alone and the remainder in combination with other drugs.[10] In 1 year there were 29,412 U.S. alcohol overdose hospitalizations of youth ages 18–24.[11]

Because the liver gives priority to removing toxins from the body, heavy drinking interferes with normal regulation of blood sugar and can cause dangerous levels of hypoglycemia, particularly in combination with diabetes or drinking on an empty stomach.[12,13] A large dose of alcohol can also disrupt heart rhythm, producing potentially life-threatening patterns of rapid or irregular heartbeat in otherwise healthy individuals.[14] This is common enough during holiday periods to have earned the name *holiday heart syndrome,* and intoxication is one cause of an unexplained sudden heart attack in people without a history of heart disease.[15]

A third kind of risk pertains to drinking in the wrong *situation,* which might be thought of as dumb drinking. There are contexts in which having any amount of alcohol poses significant potential danger; for example, during pregnancy, driving a vehicle, performing surgery, or flying an airplane. Considering the effects of various BAC levels described in Chapter 4, what are times or situations in your own life in which having alcohol in your body has been or would be unwise? Remember that once alcohol is in your bloodstream, it takes time for your body to remove it. A very rough guideline is that it takes about an hour to process one standard drink, but, as we explain in Chapter 7, this varies a lot by body weight and gender.

Because eliminating alcohol from the body takes time, it can also happen that a risky situation occurs *after* drinking. For example, you might have a few drinks before an unexpected circumstance arises. This happened to a mother who had urged her children to call her from a party rather than accepting a ride with a driver who had been drinking.

The mother herself had been drinking when her daughter phoned asking to be picked up. Rather than driving, she arranged for a friend to get her daughter home safely. In another case, a father was surprised to discover during his checkup that he was drinking enough during the evening so that on many mornings he was still legally intoxicated while driving his children to school.

Risky alcohol use may *not yet* have caused harm to you or others. Some people, for example, drive after drinking quite a few times before being arrested.[16] For others, even one occasion of unwise drinking has tragic consequences.

STEP 3. BAC LEVEL

In Chapter 4 we described the typical effects at various levels of blood alcohol concentration (BAC). Many drinkers, however, do not know how their own alcohol use translates into BAC. Furthermore, people who have inherited or developed tolerance to alcohol lack internal cues for intoxication. When asking people who came for a checkup or treatment, "How do you know when you have had too much to drink?" we found that their first clue might be stumbling when they got up from a chair or barstool. They didn't notice earlier signs that alcohol was affecting them.

It is useful, then, to know what your BAC is likely to be from various amounts of alcohol. Several websites can help you estimate BAC. For example, by entering your gender and body weight at ***https://casaa.unm.edu/assets/html/bac.html,*** you can create a table that shows your estimated BAC with a certain number of standard drinks over a period of up to 10 hours. The table on the facing page shows a sample BAC table from this website for a male weighing 160 pounds. In the left column, find six standard drinks, then find expected BAC levels after various lengths of time. The zero (0) column shows what his BAC might

Sample BAC Estimation Table for 160-Pound Male

NUMBER OF HOURS	NUMBER OF STANDARD DRINKS										
0	0	1	2	3	4	5	6	7	8	9	10
1	23	7	0	0	0	0	0	0	0	0	0
2	47	31	15	0	0	0	0	0	0	0	0
3	70	54	38	22	6	0	0	0	0	0	0
4	94	78	62	46	30	14	0	0	0	0	0
5	117	101	85	69	53	37	21	5	0	0	0
6	141	125	109	93	77	61	45	29	13	0	0
7	164	148	132	116	100	84	68	52	36	20	4
8	188	172	156	140	124	108	92	76	60	43	27
9	211	195	179	163	147	131	115	99	83	67	51
10	234	218	202	186	170	154	138	122	106	90	74
11	258	242	226	210	194	178	162	146	130	114	98
12	281	265	249	233	217	201	185	169	153	137	121
13	305	289	273	257	241	225	209	193	177	161	145
14	328	312	296	280	264	248	232	216	200	184	168
15	352	336	320	304	288	272	256	240	224	208	192
16	375	359	343	327	311	295	279	263	247	231	215
17	398	382	366	350	334	318	302	286	270	254	238
18	422	406	390	374	358	342	326	310	294	278	262
19	445	429	413	397	381	365	349	333	317	301	285
20	469	453	437	421	405	389	373	357	341	325	309
21	492	476	460	444	428	412	396	380	364	348	332
22	516	500	484	468	452	436	420	404	388	372	356
23	539	523	507	491	475	459	443	427	411	395	379
24	563	547	531	515	499	483	467	451	435	419	402
25	586	570	554	538	522	506	490	474	458	442	426

be if this amount of ethyl alcohol were immediately in his bloodstream (.141). If he consumed those six drinks (for example, six 12-ounce beers) over a period of 2 hours, his BAC would be about .109. If he drank nothing else, his BAC at 4 hours (2 hours later) would still be .077, and it would take 5 more hours to completely clear alcohol from his body.

You can create a personal table based on your gender and body weight. The same website offers another tool that allows you to enter amounts of different kinds of alcoholic beverages consumed in a specific amount of time, and it computes the number of standard drinks as well as an estimate of your likely BAC level: *https://casaa.unm.edu/tools/baccalc.html.*

We emphasize that these are just *estimates* of average BAC after periods of drinking.[17,18] Don't count on them to be accurate in your particular situation; they are only best guesses, and BAC can be affected by other factors, such as your age, the health of your liver, and whether you have food in your stomach. Also remember that alcohol tolerance does *not* mean that you have a lower BAC than others would; rather, it means that you're just less likely to *know* when your BAC is high.

STEP 4. HARMFUL DRINKING

As mentioned in Chapter 1, harmful drinking is occurring when alcohol is already having negative effects in your life for you, others, or your relationships. Like the amount you drink, negative consequences of alcohol use can vary from none to severe. There is really no dividing line where alcohol-related harm becomes "a problem." Just one of the consequences in the following list might be very significant for you. It's just that over time they can accumulate as drinking continues or increases. Step 4 is to reflect on this aspect of your alcohol use.

The Drinker Inventory of Consequences (DrInC) on pages 41–42 has been used in many studies.[19,20] It lists 45 things that people

Drinker's Inventory of Consequences (DrInC)[19]

Has this *ever* happened to you?

1.	I have had a hangover or felt bad after drinking.	Yes	No
2.	I have felt bad about myself because of my drinking.	Yes	No
3.	I have missed days of work or school because of my drinking.	Yes	No
4.	My family or friends have worried or complained about my drinking.	Yes	No
5.	The quality of my work has suffered because of my drinking.	Yes	No
6.	My ability to be a good parent has been harmed by my drinking.	Yes	No
7.	After drinking, I have had trouble with sleeping, staying asleep, or nightmares.	Yes	No
8.	I have driven a motor vehicle after having three or more drinks.	Yes	No
9.	My drinking has caused me to use other drugs more.	Yes	No
10.	I have been sick and vomited after drinking.	Yes	No
11.	I have been unhappy because of my drinking.	Yes	No
12.	Because of my drinking, I have not eaten properly.	Yes	No
13.	I have failed to do what is expected of me because of my drinking.	Yes	No
14.	I have felt guilty or ashamed because of my drinking.	Yes	No
15.	While drinking, I have said or done embarrassing things.	Yes	No
16.	When drinking, my personality has changed for the worse.	Yes	No
17.	I have taken foolish risks when I have been drinking.	Yes	No
18.	I have gotten into trouble because of drinking.	Yes	No
19.	While drinking, I have said harsh or cruel things to someone.	Yes	No
20.	When drinking, I have done impulsive things that I regretted later.	Yes	No
21.	I have gotten into a physical fight while drinking.	Yes	No
22.	My physical health has been harmed by my drinking.	Yes	No
23.	I have had money problems because of my drinking.	Yes	No

(continued)

Drinker's Inventory of Consequences (*continued*)

Has this *ever* happened to you?

24.	My marriage or love relationship has been harmed by my drinking.	Yes	No
25.	I have smoked tobacco more when I am drinking.	Yes	No
26.	My physical appearance has been harmed by my drinking.	Yes	No
27.	My family has been hurt by my drinking.	Yes	No
28.	A friendship or close relationship has been damaged by my drinking.	Yes	No
29.	I have been overweight because of my drinking.	Yes	No
30.	My sex life has suffered because of my drinking.	Yes	No
31.	I have lost interest in activities and hobbies because of my drinking.	Yes	No
32.	My spiritual or moral life has been harmed by my drinking.	Yes	No
33.	Because of my drinking, I have not had the kind of life that I want.	Yes	No
34.	My drinking has gotten in the way of my growth as a person.	Yes	No
35.	My drinking has damaged my social life, popularity, or reputation.	Yes	No
36.	I have spent too much or lost a lot of money because of my drinking.	Yes	No
37.	I have been arrested for driving under the influence of alcohol.	Yes	No
38.	I have had trouble with the law (other than driving while intoxicated) because of my drinking.	Yes	No
39.	I have lost a marriage or a close love relationship because of my drinking.	Yes	No
40.	I have been suspended/fired from or left a job or school because of my drinking.	Yes	No
41.	I have lost a friend because of my drinking.	Yes	No
42.	I have had an accident while drinking or intoxicated.	Yes	No
43.	While drinking or intoxicated, I have been physically hurt, injured, or burned.	Yes	No
44.	While drinking or intoxicated, I have injured someone else.	Yes	No
45.	I have broken things while drinking or intoxicated.	Yes	No

sometimes experience during or after drinking. It can be used to count things that have happened recently (for example, within the past 3 months), but the version here asks which ones you have *ever* experienced. If an item is something that has *ever* occurred in your lifetime, circle or highlight *yes*. If it has never happened or does not apply to you, circle or highlight *no*. If you don't want to write in this book, keep a separate list of the item numbers for which you answered *yes*. This is just a personal inventory and will not result in a label or diagnosis. Please do this now before continuing the chapter.

Now, before proceeding, add up the number of items for which you answered *yes* and record it here ______ or on your separate sheet. That is your DrInC score.

As promised, we won't give you a label or diagnosis. What we can offer is an opportunity to compare your own score with two large samples of drinkers. The first (see the box on page 44) is a group of 1,674 people who voluntarily completed an anonymous online drinker's checkup that included the DrInC questionnaire.[21] The fact that they all signed up for this checkup means that this is far from a random sample of adults. They already had enough concern about their drinking to seek a checkup, and in fact their alcohol use was far above average (the men reported having 26 standard drinks per week on average, and the women 20 drinks per week). The box shows their average lifetime scores on the DrInC questionnaire, ranging from the lowest to the highest 10%.[21]

As you can see, there was little difference between men and women in their lifetime DrInC scores. The men were consuming more alcohol than the women were (26 versus 20 drinks per week), but, as we have discussed, women reach higher BACs when drinking the same amount as men do.

Another group with whom you can compare your own score consists of 1,726 people enrolled in treatment for alcohol use disorders (see the box on page 45). They were being treated in a large clinical trial known as Project MATCH.[4] As you might expect, people who were already receiving treatment were very heavy drinkers (about 60 standard drinks per week on average) and had more severe alcohol problems than those who were just seeking a drinker's checkup. Our experience has been that drinkers are, in fact, receptive to a checkup well before they are willing to enter formal treatment.[1,2] By the time they entered this alcohol treatment program, they had accumulated substantially more adverse lifetime consequences of their drinking. We believe that this is due partly to the fact that substance use disorders are often treated in stigmatized specialist programs rather than in routine health care.[22,23]

People Receiving a Drinker's Checkup

		Lifetime Consequences of Drinking (DrInC Score)[19]	
	Decile	*Men*	*Women*
Highest	10	35–45	35–45
	9	32–34	32–34
	8	29–31	28–31
	7	26–28	26–27
	6	24–25	23–25
	5	21–23	21–22
	4	19–20	19–20
	3	16–18	16–18
	2	13–15	13–15
Lowest	1	0–12	0–12

People in Treatment for Alcohol Use Disorder

	Decile	Lifetime Consequences of Drinking (DrInC Score)[19] Men	Women
Highest	10	43–45	42–45
	9	41–42	39–41
	8	39–40	37–38
	7	37–38	35–36
	6	36	32–34
	5	33–35	29–31
	4	31–32	26–28
	3	28–30	24–25
	2	23–27	19–23
Lowest	1	0–22	0–18

Here, again, are lifetime scores from the DrInC questionnaire for groups ranging from the lowest 10% to the highest 10% of patients in treatment. You can compare your own lifetime consequences score with those of people seeking a drinker's checkup and those already receiving treatment.

STEP 5. REASONS FOR DRINKING

Step 5 considers your own motivations for drinking that you considered in Chapter 2. Of the "Big Six" groups of common reasons, which ones are important for you? If you haven't completed it yet, please do so now. Pages 12–14 in Chapter 2 give more detail about these reasons. Give each group of motivations a letter indicating its importance for you: A, B, C, or D. It's okay to use the same letter more than once.

A	Definitely! That's important for me.
B	Mostly that's true for me.
C	That matters a little—it's somewhat true for me.
D	Not at all. That's definitely not a reason why I drink.

		Importance letter
1	**Enjoyment:** taste, feeling of a drink or two, fun occasions	
2	**Relationships:** fitting in, being polite, being expected to drink	
3	**Socializing:** to feel more relaxed, outgoing, at ease, aroused, confident	
4	**Relief:** to cope, make unpleasant experiences go away	
5	**Being drunk:** enjoying being drunk, having a break from being sober	
6	**Necessity:** have to drink to feel normal, relieve hangover or withdrawal	

It does matter *why* you drink. Research shows that the reasons with a *higher* number in this list are generally associated with more drinking and greater risk for significant harm and problems. Drinking solely to enjoy the taste or the feeling of a drink or two is usually associated with less drinking and lower risk of alcohol-related problems.[24] That's also true for people who *dislike* the taste and effects of alcohol.

Relationship and socializing motivations for alcohol use represent, on average, a step up in amount of drinking. For adolescents, relationship reasons (e.g., to fit in) are often more important than drinking for relief, at least in their early drinking years.[24] Socializing reasons are one example of drinking to change how you feel—to relieve social discomfort.[24] Relief drinking to cope with negative feelings is an example of relying or depending on alcohol and is associated with heavier drinking and more severe problems and consequences.[24–27] Using alcohol to forget problems and personal shortcomings is often related to solitary drinking.[28]

Drinking to get drunk (inebriation) is, like memory blackouts, associated with still higher levels of alcohol use, intoxication, and more severe consequences. Note that going for a higher blood alcohol level is sometimes what is meant by drinking for "fun," but it's quite different from enjoyment drinking for taste or early effects.[29] Finally, experiences of necessity—craving or urges, drinking to relieve a hangover or feel normal—happen with higher intoxication levels and indicate physical addiction to alcohol.[30,31]

STEP 6. ALCOHOL DEPENDENCE

If alcohol use continues to progress over time, drinkers can grow increasingly dependent on alcohol as a drug. They begin to rely on having alcohol and become uncomfortable without it. A sixth and final part of this personal checkup considers to what extent this may be happening with you.

Psychological dependence is one form of reliance on alcohol. It happens when alcohol is the only or primary way you have to respond to life's challenges. Think of alcohol as one way to get from a less to a more desirable place. Reasons for drinking (Step 5) are important here.[30,32] Some more specific examples of situations in which relief drinking may occur are:

- Being angry, frustrated, sad, or bored
- Experiencing physical or emotional pain
- Conflict or tension in a relationship
- Being criticized
- Feeling lonely or left out

When you rely on alcohol as the only way you have to get from a less pleasant to a more pleasant state, you really don't have a choice. Discomfort is going to happen. To have freedom of choice, you need other ways to respond, new roads for getting to where you want to be.[33] Part Four of this book is all about finding those alternate routes.

Physical dependence is the most severe type of alcohol disorder, in which the body grows so accustomed to alcohol being present that it reacts badly when it's not. The familiar pattern is alcohol withdrawal, ranging from mild hangovers to severe and potentially life-threatening reactions. Only about 10% of people who came for a drinker's checkup reported having experiences like these on the day after drinking alcohol:

I dreaded waking up in the morning.

I felt very frightened when I awoke.

I had a very strong craving for alcohol when I awoke.

I liked to have an alcoholic drink in the morning.

I was afraid to meet people first thing in the morning.

I woke up feeling sweaty.

I woke up absolutely drenched in sweat.

My hands shook the first thing in the morning.

My whole body shook violently first thing in the morning if I didn't have a drink.

I drank more alcohol in the morning to get rid of the shakes.

I felt at the edge of despair when I awoke.

I always gulped my first few alcoholic drinks down as quickly as possible.

If you are experiencing some of these withdrawal symptoms, you are like people who were already receiving treatment for alcohol use disorders. Consult with your primary health care provider about available options.

MOVING ON

Now that you have taken time to reflect on these six aspects of your alcohol use, it's time to consider where you want to go from here. Chapter 6 is about choosing your own way by setting goals, offering you some tools to help in decision making. Then, if you decide that you want to continue using alcohol but make some changes in how you drink, Part Three is for you. Whatever you decide, to drink or not to drink, Part Four offers some life skills you can use instead of depending on alcohol.

6

CHOOSING YOUR OWN WAY

So far in this book we've discussed changing social views and practices on drinking and given you information about how alcohol works in the body. We've also helped you consider your reasons for drinking and not drinking and offered an opportunity for a personal checkup. What are you thinking about drinking at this point? What changes, if any, are you considering? Choosing the path that you want to try is your next step. Before getting down to specifics, here are our own two stories in brief. Feel free to skip over them and get right to your own story. You could always come back to our stories later if you're so inclined.

BILL: WHY I DRINK MODERATELY

I grew up in a working-class teetotaling home. My parents both abstained from alcohol, though they never explained why. Our church did not totally prohibit alcohol; it was just the norm not to drink, and communion always involved grape juice rather than wine. My German grandfather, with whom we lived, kept a bottle of sweet wine, and he sometimes made his own wine from the grapes that grew in our backyard. His bottle of wine lasted for a long time, and I don't think I ever saw him actually drinking, certainly not intoxicated.

The legal drinking age in Pennsylvania was 21. I was 22 and in college before I drank any kind of alcoholic beverage. It was wine at first, and I didn't particularly appreciate the taste. I've always disliked the taste of beer and of coffee, too, for that matter. I tried some mixed drinks in college and didn't enjoy the effects, so I never really was a capital-D Drinker.

After my second year of graduate school, I went on a summer internship at the Veterans Administration hospital in Milwaukee, Wisconsin. The psychology training director told me to visit the various units to see where I might like to spend the summer. There was an inpatient alcoholism treatment program directed by a clinical psychologist, who asked me, "What do you know about alcoholism?"

"Nothing," I replied.

"No family history?"

"Not that I know of."

"Well, what did you hear about alcoholism in your graduate psychology courses?"

"Honestly, I don't remember it ever coming up."

"Well," he said, "this is the first or second most common diagnosis that you're likely to encounter as a psychologist. You might want to learn something about it."

So I did. I enjoyed talking with patients on the unit, and I wound up devoting much of my career to treating substance use disorders. In the course of reading about alcohol that summer, I realized that I had been drinking more than was good for me. A common screening question in primary care today is, "When was the last time you had five or more drinks on one occasion?" For me it's now over 50 years.

I did learn to enjoy wines, particularly with a good meal. A federal health guideline for men has been to have no more than two drinks a day, and not every day. For me, two glasses of wine with dinner is now pretty much my maximum, and that's usually just one or two days a week. Sometimes I'll have a different drink with my wife. I did once believe that there were health benefits from moderate drinking, and we said so in our previous book.[1] As I read current scientific research, the risk of having my usual amount of alcohol is not significantly different from zero. For now, I'm content to enjoy the taste of a good wine with dinner or an occasional drink of another kind. I am also open to rethinking this over time.

RICARDO: WHY I DON'T DRINK

I grew up in a household that used alcohol during social occasions. My father had a shelf with whiskey, wine, pisco, and champagne bottles in our dining room. When we were children or adolescents, we were allowed to have a taste of these during birthdays and other celebratory events, though the alcohol bottles were always accessible to us. In fact, one day, when I was in high school, I had stayed home from school because I had a bad cold. My best friend's mother called to see if he was with me, and when I told her I had a bad cold and a sore throat, she suggested that some alcohol might help. So, I took a regular water glass and filled it to the top with straight whiskey. I began drinking it and found that it was hard to swallow, but, thinking that it would be good for my cold, I went ahead and forced down the whole glass. I remember feeling a bit giddy at first and gradually kind of dazed or benumbed. My father was very angry with me when he came home. I imagine I must have looked very much under the influence.

I lived in a dorm in college from 1968 to 1972. At the time, when the dorm would get together on weekends, it was not unusual for a joint to be passed around. I would regularly take the joint and pass it on without smoking it. One day, the guy who had handed me the joint, upon seeing me pass it on without taking a toke, asked me if I ever used pot. I said I did not. Then he asked me if I drank alcohol. I said I did. He then said, "You know, alcohol is much more harmful than marijuana. And if you don't believe me, look it up!" So I did.

I went to the university library and began reading articles on the health effects of alcohol and marijuana. And I found out the guy was right. Even back then it was already clear that alcohol has the many harmful medical, behavioral, and social effects described in Chapter 4. Obviously, my dorm mate had intended for me to see that alcohol, which I was accustomed to using, was much more dangerous than marijuana and that, therefore, using marijuana should be okay with me. My conclusion, however, was that I should stop using alcohol. It just did not make sense to me to use something that had so many negative consequences.

Being in social situations where alcohol was available (and back then, it seemed to be always available, at least at the social situations I attended) and not accepting drinks was, at first, a bit uncomfortable. I felt I had to explain why I was not drinking. Some friends clearly felt offended at my not joining in. Much later, at professional events, even medical professionals would express disapproval at my not partaking of some wine, for example. Eventually I stopped explaining why I was not drinking and found that most people did not even notice.

My own not drinking seems to have had an impact on my family. In none of my immediate family's reunions is alcohol usually served. Sometimes a person may bring their own bottle. My wife and I did not have alcohol at our wedding. We do not worry about our children having alcohol problems. And we have probably saved a lot of money over the years. We are amazed at how expensive alcoholic drinks can be.

I believe individuals have the right to take risks with their lives, so I do not try to persuade people to stop using alcohol. I am happy to explain why I do not, if asked. I have become aware that my not drinking can be supportive of other people who do not drink, including people who abstain because they have had problems related to using alcohol. And I have noticed that at many stores and social events there are now tasty nonalcoholic drinks. Overall, I feel quite comfortable with what I consider a personal choice not to use alcohol.

YOUR OWN STORY

People are always changing. Chances are that what and how you drink has varied over the years and will continue to change. In our own work as clinical psychologists, we have been fascinated to witness how much people can and do change over time. One reason that I (Bill) have continued focusing on addiction treatment for 50 years is that, contrary to public impressions, the outcomes are so *good*. In this field, it is possible to measure reliably whether alcohol/drug use and related problems have decreased.[2,3] Not only do most people recover, but their lives are far better in so many ways that you don't even need subtle psychological measures to see it.

People do things impulsively, but in the long run choices are a matter of weighing the pros and cons, the benefits and risks.[4–6] There are plenty of activities that involve taking some risk: driving a car or truck, making an investment, going on a date, flying in an airplane, or walking near traffic. People voluntarily take risks that may require a signed waiver: bungee jumping, surgery, or riding a mule down the Grand Canyon. Rethinking drinking is about comparing the positives and negatives of alcohol for you.

How *important* is drinking to you now? On the following rating scale, how important would you say that alcohol is in your life if 0 means "not at all" and 10 means "very important; one of the most important things in my life"?

0	1	2	3	4	5	6	7	8	9	10
Not at all										Very important

It's really up to you. No one else can decide this for you. You could decide any of these:

- "I'm going to drink even more."
- "I'm not changing how I use alcohol at all."
- "I choose to decrease my alcohol use."
- "I plan to try not drinking for a while and see what it's like."
- "I'm going to decide now to be a nondrinker."

The choice you make is likely to have important effects on your health and the quality of your life. Whichever of these you choose to try, it's possible to change your mind later and make a different decision based on your experience.

Now using the same 10-point rating scale, given what you have learned so far, how important would you say it is for you to *decrease* your drinking, whether that would involve cutting down or quitting? Zero means that it's not at all important; there's nothing you need to change. Ten means that it's very important, maybe one of the most important choices in your life.

0	1	2	3	4	5	6	7	8	9	10
Not at all										Very important

Circle (or highlight) one number, at least mentally.

Why did you choose that number instead of zero? We think it's worth your while not just to *think* about this, but actually to write down your reasons here or on a separate sheet.

____

____

____

____

____

TO BE A MODERATE DRINKER OR NONDRINKER

People who came to our research clinic knew they were drinking too much and were hoping to reduce and manage their use of alcohol. Most had not received any prior treatment for alcohol problems. They were curious about how moderation would work for them, and so were we.

Over the years, our research was full of surprises. We started out helping people learn how to control their drinking.[7] These were heavier drinkers who had been having 40 or more standard drinks per week. On average, people cut their drinking in half, but after seven studies in 10 years we found that more people had quit drinking altogether rather than maintaining moderation.[8] We had thought that might happen if people tried to moderate their drinking and failed, therefore deciding that they had to quit. That's not what happened. Instead, the ultimate abstainers had *succeeded* in reducing their drinking and then told us that it was difficult to maintain and that they didn't see any point in drinking so little. In other words, they were working hard without enjoying it, so they decided it was just easier to quit, and they did. Others maintained moderate drinking for years, and some were still struggling despite our efforts to help them.

Another unexpected finding occurred because our studies included a comparison group who were given our self-help book and told to go home and follow the instructions, with a promise to see them 2 or 3 months later to see how they were doing. We thought they might be disappointed when they were assigned to this self-help group rather than immediately seeing a therapist, but in fact many were pleasantly surprised that they could work on their own. On average, in four different clinical trials, those randomly assigned to use the self-help book were just as successful in reducing their alcohol use as those seen by a therapist using the same methods.[9–12] Our self-help guidelines are those described in Parts Three and Four of this book.

Finally, there are some specific conditions in which even moderate drinking can be hazardous:

- If you are pregnant or might become pregnant, because alcohol is dangerous to an unborn child from the day of conception, and there is no known safe level of drinking during pregnancy.
- If you have a medical condition (such as liver disease or a stomach ulcer) that could be made worse by any drinking. Your physician should evaluate this. If you have not had a thorough physical examination recently, we strongly recommend that you do so before making decisions about alcohol use.
- If you tend to lose control of your behavior (e.g., tend to become aggressive or violent) when you drink even small amounts of alcohol.
- If you are taking tranquilizers, sedatives, sleeping pills, or any other medication that is dangerous when combined with alcohol. Ask your pharmacist!
- If you have had significant problems with drinking in the past and have already been refraining from alcohol successfully, we recommend that you stick with abstinence.

If you choose to reduce your drinking, go on to Part Three. It has specific steps and tips for reducing alcohol use that have been tested in more than 50 years of research by ourselves and others.[13–16] No matter what you decide, whether to be a moderate drinker or a nondrinker, Part Four is for you. It offers ways to enjoy a good life without having to depend on alcohol.

Part Three

MAKING THE CHANGES YOU WANT

7

SETTING SENSIBLE LIMITS

An important first step in making any intentional change is to have a clear goal in mind. Setting limits for yourself is perhaps the simplest strategy for managing your drinking, and it's often the first thing that people try. It's a bit like setting your home thermostat to keep the temperature within the range you choose.

What should your own goals be? That's up to you, of course. Here is some information to help you decide.

KNOW WHAT YOU'RE DRINKING

As we explained in Chapter 5, all alcoholic beverages contain the same chemical, ethanol, so from the strength of what you are drinking you can know exactly how much alcohol you have consumed. There is an international consensus that one "standard drink" equals 0.6 ounce (17.7 milliliters) of ethanol—the amount in 12 ounces of beer (5% alcohol), 5 ounces of wine (12%), or 1½ ounces of 80-proof liquor (40%). Remember, though, that alcoholic beverages can vary widely in their alcohol content, so check the label and know what you're drinking.

A number of online tools are available to help you calculate the number of standard units in what you drink, such as *https://standarddrinks.org/calculator* and *https://rethinkingdrinking.niaaa.nih.gov/tools/calculators/drink-size-calculator.* In Chapter 5, you estimated your typical number of standard drinks per week and were able to compare this with national averages for adults.

A REGULAR LIMIT

We recommend choosing some specific goals. The first one is a *regular* limit—the maximum number of drinks that you choose to have per day and per week. (We'll consider special occasions shortly.) Take into account the information presented in prior chapters, including the recommended daily limits discussed in Chapter 1 and the national drinking norms from Chapter 5. Based on what you know so far, what might you set as your goal for how many drinks you'll have per day and per week?

Number of standard drinks per day: ______

Number of standard drinks per week: ______

AN OCCASIONAL LIMIT

An important second goal is your *occasional* limit, a blood alcohol concentration (BAC) level above which you would choose not to go even on those occasions when you may drink more than your regular limit. Based on what you learned about the effect of BAC levels in Chapter 4 and about BAC in your own body in Chapter 5, what do you choose as your occasional limit? (Remember that if you are going to be driving, swimming, or engaging in other potentially risky activities, we do not recommend any BAC level greater than zero.)

Occasional BAC limit: ______ mg%

How can you honor this goal? Here's where you can use a personal BAC table, as mentioned in Chapter 5. If you haven't gotten one for yourself, try this free online site—*https://casaa.unm.edu/assets/html/bac.html*—by entering your sex and body weight. Across the top of your table, you will see various periods of drinking. This is the length of time (in hours) from starting the first drink to finishing the last. Down the side, you'll find the number of standard drinks, ranging from 1 to 25. Now try these three steps.

Step 1. Watching Your BAC Rise

On your table, run your finger down the "1 hour" column. As you go from one standard drink to two to three and so on, you can see the BAC level that the computer projects for various amounts of drinking within 1 hour. How much does your BAC level go up with each drink? Try the same for the "2 hours" column.

Step 2. Watching Your BAC Drop

Next run your finger along the row for four standard drinks. If you had four standard drinks in 1 hour, what would your BAC level be? Now, moving to the right, what if you spread the same four drinks over 2 hours? Over 3 hours? Over 4 hours? How much does your BAC drop with each hour? This is also how you can estimate how long it would take for your BAC level to get down to zero after having had a certain number of drinks. Regardless of how sober you feel, we strongly recommend that you allow your BAC level to drop all the way to zero before driving, swimming, boating, using machinery, or doing anything else that is potentially dangerous. Some people in our clinic were surprised, at this step, to discover that even after they have "slept off" an evening's drinking, their BAC could still be high the next morning.

Step 3. Honoring Your Limit

Now use your table to translate your occasional limit (the BAC level that you choose not to exceed) into standard drinks. This is the trickiest step. Using your table, what is the maximum number of standard drinks that you could have in 1 hour to stay within your chosen BAC limit? In 2 hours? In 3 hours?

An example may help. Suppose that a person chose an occasional BAC limit of 60 mg% (.06). To stay under this limit, a 180-pound (82-kilogram) man could have three drinks in 1 hour (three drinks would result in a BAC of 46 mg%, whereas four would raise his BAC to 67 mg%). If he spreads his drinks over a period of 2 hours instead of 1, he could have four drinks (BAC = 51 mg%) and still stay under his occasional limit. Similarly, he could have only five drinks over 3 hours (56 mg%), and, even over a period of 4 hours, six drinks would still put him just over his limit (61 mg%).

Compare the numbers for a 140-pound (65-kilogram) woman. For her to stay at or under a BAC of 60, her limits would be:

Two drinks in 1 hour (48 mg%)

Two drinks in 2 hours (32 mg%)

Three drinks in 3 hours (48 mg%)

Three drinks in 4 hours (32 mg%)

Even a 180-pound (80-kilogram) woman, with the same body weight as the man mentioned previously, would have lower limits than those for the man:

Three drinks in 1 hour (59 mg%)

Three drinks in 2 hours (43 mg%)

Four drinks in 3 hours (52 mg%)

Four drinks in 4 hours (36 mg%)

Now try it for your own table. For your own occasional BAC limit of______ mg%, what is the maximum number of standard drinks you could have and still stay within your limit during:

1 hour of drinking? ____ standard drinks

2 hours of drinking? ____ standard drinks

3 hours of drinking? ____ standard drinks

4 hours of drinking? ____ standard drinks

5 hours of drinking? ____ standard drinks

We must emphasize that these tables estimate *average* BAC levels for men and women. Of course, people do differ from each other, and these tables will not be exactly right for any one individual. Your BAC is influenced by other factors, such as how recently you've eaten, your stage in the menstrual cycle, the mood you are in, your age and the health of your liver, and even your genetic makeup. We certainly can't guarantee what your BAC level will be. Still, these tables are useful in setting goals, because they give you a best guess about BAC levels you can expect to reach with different quantities of alcohol. In addition to the amount you drink, they take into account these three important factors: your sex, your weight, and the amount of time you take to finish the drinks.

Notice another important fact: The number of drinks you can consume per hour and still stay within your limit decreases with each hour. Being able to have three drinks in 1 hour does not mean you can have six in 2 hours. Once you're up to your maximum BAC, it takes (for most people) less than one standard drink per hour to stay there. This is because the liver can break down only a small amount of alcohol each hour, and, as you continue to drink, alcohol keeps building up in your bloodstream.

"CAN'T I JUST TELL FROM HOW I FEEL?"

Something that we tried in our research clinic was teaching people how to know their BAC level from their bodily sensations. As people drank, we used a breath analyzer to give feedback of their actual BAC while they attended to their own bodily feelings. Some people can learn to do this, but ironically those who need it most seem to be the least able to learn it. Heavier drinkers are often unable to learn how to judge their intoxication level from how they are feeling, even with biofeedback and training. In contrast, estimating BAC levels by counting drinks can work for anyone, regardless of how much they drink. That's why we recommend using a BAC estimation table. If your weight changes substantially, go online to get another BAC table for your new weight.

SOBERING UP: TRUE OR FALSE?

How can you lower your BAC more quickly or keep the alcohol you consume from taking effect? Circle or highlight "True" or "False" for each of the following statements.

1. Coffee or vitamins or other drugs will decrease the impact of alcohol. ____ True ____ False
2. You will not get as drunk if you avoid mixing different kinds of drinks. ____ True ____ False
3. You won't get as drunk on beer. ____ True ____ False
4. Exercise gets rid of alcohol more quickly.
   ____ True ____ False

All of these beliefs are myths.

1. **False.** A stimulant such as coffee does not cancel out the effect of a depressant. Instead, you have a "wide-awake drunk."
2. **False.** What matters is the total amount of alcohol you consume. You get just as drunk on six 12-ounce (355 milliliters) beers as you would on two beers plus 6 ounces (177 milliliters) of 80-proof liquor, assuming you drink them over the same period.
3. **False.** Remember that a 12-ounce can of beer (at 5% alcohol) contains more alcohol than an ounce of 100-proof liquor. A majority of the accidental deaths and injuries, chronic illnesses, and social problems related to alcohol in the United States are consequences of beer drinking.
4. **False.** Exercise does not speed up the rate at which alcohol is eliminated from the body.

Only two things can help to keep you from getting drunk:

1. **Eat before and during drinking.** Having food in the stomach decreases the speed with which alcohol is absorbed into the bloodstream. Drinking on an empty stomach increases the impact of alcohol

because it goes directly into the bloodstream and on to the brain. The longer alcohol stays in the stomach, the more it can be broken down before it gets into the blood (particularly in men). Oily foods that coat the stomach (such as olive oil) work best. Huge doses of fructose (fruit sugar) do speed up alcohol metabolism, but you're unlikely to be able to eat enough fruit to make a difference. Certainly a fruit juice mixer won't save you.

2. **Drink moderately.** This is, of course, the surest preventive measure against intoxication.

REMEMBER YOUR LIMITS

We found that one of the first things people usually have tried in managing their drinking is to set specific limits for themselves. That is a good first step. This chapter was designed to help you set sensible limits, informed by knowledge about drinking and how alcohol affects people. Now put your goals all in one place, using the Personal Goals Card on the facing page (or make a card of your own). You first set a regular limit (page 62), the number of standard drinks that you chose as your upper limit for most weeks when you drink. What was it? Record it on your Personal Goals Card.

Then you also selected a BAC level that you choose not to exceed even on occasional days when you may go over your regular limit (page 63). Record your occasional BAC limit on the Personal Goals Card.

Finally, using your BAC estimation table, you translated this into a maximum number of drinks you would have in various lengths of time and still remain within your occasional limit (page 65). Record these on your Personal Goals Card on the facing page.

Before moving on, take one more look at the goals you've set for yourself. Do they seem reasonable? Is that what you want to shoot for,

Personal Goals Card

My regular limit: ____ standard drinks per day

My occasional BAC limit: ____ mg%

____ standard drinks in 1 hour

or ____ standard drinks in 2 hours

or ____ standard drinks in 3 hours

or ____ standard drinks in 4 hours

or ____ standard drinks in 5 hours

at least for now? If so, give it a try! You're always free, of course, to revise your goals upward or downward later.

Once you have clear goals set for yourself, the next challenge is how to stick with them. *Everything else in the chapters that follow is designed to help you reach your goal of self-control within these limits.* It's up to you to decide how best to reach your goal, choosing from the menu of methods that we suggest or trying out your own ideas. There is a pleasant side to this responsibility, too. Any change that occurs in your drinking is clearly your own accomplishment. Success in using self-control methods is *your* success. That's why it's called *self*-control.

8

KEEPING TRACK

To learn most any skill or accomplish an intentional change, you need at least two things: a clear goal and accurate feedback about how you're doing. Chapter 7 focused on the goal. Now it's time to give yourself reliable feedback. It's very hard to practice archery in the dark: You may shoot a lot of arrows, but you're not likely to get much better at hitting the target unless you can see where your shots land. Learning requires good feedback. That's what this chapter is about.

This step is fairly simple. You need to start keeping track of your drinking—keeping good records of your alcohol use, much as you would use a checkbook or financial software to keep track of your use of money. Keeping good records is far better than occasionally thinking about what you've done and trying to guess how you are doing. When you keep good track of your drinking, you know for sure. Psychologists refer to keeping records of what you do as *self-monitoring.*

There are three good reasons to start self-monitoring now.

1. First and foremost, you need accurate feedback. When you count your drinks, you know for sure whether you are moving in the

right direction. It's right there in black and white, and there is no fooling yourself about it. Either you are moving toward your goal or you are not.

2. Self-monitoring in itself seems to help people reduce their drinking. When we asked people who made successful changes what they had found to be most helpful, the one thing they mentioned most often was keeping these records. They said things like:

> "It helped me be more aware of my drinking, to pay attention."
>
> "The cards caused me to think about it each time before I took a drink."
>
> "Keeping these records, I couldn't kid myself. It was right there in front of me."

3. The self-monitoring method described here also leads to self-discovery, helping you learn more about your own drinking. The records you have kept will be very useful in helping you analyze situations in which you may overdrink.

Remember that this is *self*-monitoring—something that you do on your own, for yourself.

So what is involved in self-monitoring? It requires carrying a small card and something to write with or an electronic device that lets you keep records. The system that we recommend for keeping track of your drinking looks like the form on page 72.

You can make a simple version of this on standard 3" × 5" lined index cards (available at many retail outlets and online) just by writing a few words across the top and drawing vertical lines to divide the columns. Either create a supply of these by hand, make one and photocopy it onto card stock, or print them from a computer. You may be using quite a few of them while you rethink your drinking.

Daily Record Card

Date	Time	Type of drink	Amount	Situation

Then get used to carrying your record cards around with you all the time. Put them (or the digital device where you've set up this record) in a convenient place such as your pocket, purse, wallet, or checkbook. Once you've done this, you are ready to start self-monitoring.

HOW TO USE SELF-MONITORING CARDS

The rule for effective self-monitoring is fairly simple: *Every* time that you have *any* alcohol beverage *anywhere,* write it on your card *before you drink it.* As the card illustrated here indicates, there are five things to write down, at least in abbreviated form, every time you have a drink: (1) the *date* and (2) *time,* (3) the *kind* and (4) *amount* of the drink, and

(5) something about the *situation* in which you are drinking. Now for the practicalities.

Know What You're Drinking

To keep good records of your alcohol use, you have to know what you're drinking. In particular, you need to know how much alcohol there is in the drink in your hand. This requires that you know two things: how many ounces of beverage you have and what percentage of alcohol it contains.

Ounces

When you're drinking a beverage from a commercial can or bottle, the size is usually indicated on the label. If you encounter unfamiliar measures, you can convert liquid measures between ounces and metric units:

1 liter (1,000 milliliters) = 33.8 fluid ounces

1 fluid ounce = approximately 30 milliliters, which means that

1 standard drink (0.6 oz.) = about 18 milliliters of ethyl alcohol

It becomes a little trickier when beverages are poured into a glass. If there are certain glasses that you tend to drink from at home, fill them up as you usually do, and then pour the contents into a measuring cup (minus any ice if you use it). When pouring distilled spirits, use a measuring cup. A shot glass is okay if you know how much it contains when filled to the line or rim. Bar glasses vary quite a bit in size, but your server or bartender will know how much alcohol a drink contains: "Could you please tell me how much alcohol is in the margarita?" Most servers and bartenders are concerned about their customers' safety and will be glad to give you accurate information. Avoid "topping up" your glass, because that makes it harder to keep track of how much you are drinking. Just put your hand over the top and say "No thanks" until you've finished the drink you have. (If you're afraid of appearing rude, some ideas for refusing drinks courteously and comfortably are given in Chapter 10.)

Percentage

The other thing you need to know is how much alcohol the beverage contains. In the United States, manufacturers of wine and liquor are required to list on the label the amount of alcohol in the beverage. For wine, this is typically listed as a percentage of alcohol content, which for table wines is usually somewhere between 9 and 14%. If you have to guess with a table wine, use the average of 12%. However, some wines, called *fortified wines,* are stronger. These include vermouth, port, sherry, brandy, and cognac. Again the alcohol content varies, averaging around 20%. Check the label.

With a few exceptions, distilled spirits (liquor) tend to contain between 40 and 50% alcohol. The term *proof* in the United States is a number that is simply double the percentage of alcohol, so that 86-proof whiskey contains 43% alcohol, and 100 proof is half alcohol. Sipping liqueurs vary widely, but again the alcohol content must be specified on the label. A few specialty spirits such as absinthe traditionally have very high alcohol content, as much as 75% ethanol.

That leaves beer. So far, there is no national requirement for U.S. manufacturers and distributors to specify how strong a beer is in terms of alcohol content, although some states may require it. Most standard brands in the United States contain about 5% alcohol, so as an average that is a reasonable guess. Some (but not all) light beers contain less alcohol (about 4.2%), and certain brands can contain 10–12% alcohol, overlapping with wines. These days, the burgeoning number of so-called craft beers often do state the alcohol content, and many beers exceed the average of 5%. You can find the strength of specific brands on websites like *www.findmeabrewery.com/beer-alcohol-content* and *www.alcoholcontents.com.*

A real problem emerges if you have a drink of unknown strength, such as when someone mixes it for you in another room or you drink a punch of unknown content. In general, it's best to avoid this situation. Ask to mix your own drink if that's possible or watch it being done. Find out how much of what beverages are in the punch bowl or avoid mystery punches altogether.

Writing It Down

As much as possible, it's best to have about one standard drink at a time. Some examples of this would be a 12-ounce glass of beer, a 5-ounce glass of wine, or about 1.5 ounces of distilled spirits. If you're writing down amounts like "Beer—6 pack" or "Vodka—pint," you're having too much at a time, and chances are you're writing it down afterward. Break it up into one-drink units and remember to write it down just *before* you start each drink.

Notice that in addition to type of drink and amount, the daily record card has columns for:

Date: the date on which you are having the drink

Time: the time of day when you take the first sip of the drink

Situation: for keeping track of additional information that may be important, such as where or with whom you are drinking

With a little practice, you'll be able to write all this information on your card or in your phone within a few seconds.

It's important to get into the habit of writing this information down *just before* you take the first sip of your drink. If you do it this way, the record keeping helps you be more aware of your drinking. If you wait until later to write down the information, you'll be losing much of the potential benefit of this self-control method. If you end up not finishing a drink, you can always change the entry for amount.

It can be a bit of a challenge to keep track while you're drinking, but this is an important first step in getting a handle on your use of alcohol. If you have trouble getting started with faithful record keeping, the following are some things that people have done to remind or motivate themselves.

- Make it a rule never to take a drink before recording it, and think of the first sip as your reward for writing it down.

- Figure out a good reminder for yourself—something you'll see just before you drink and that you can use to remind yourself to keep notes. Some possibilities are a small stone in your pocket or a card in your wallet that you will see when you reach for money; a note in the display on your cell phone (use a code word if you don't want to announce what you're doing to anyone who sees your phone); a ribbon on your bottle; a note on your refrigerator; a special glass or coaster that you use when drinking.

- Each time you write down a drink before starting it, say something encouraging to yourself, such as "Good," "Way to go," or "I'm really sticking to my goals."

- Involve other people in your record keeping. Someone you trust can help you remember to write down your drinks and can encourage you to do so. Don't ask this person to *police* you—it's your responsibility to keep the records—but it can be helpful if someone else understands what you're doing and encourages you.

Like most habits, once you get into the pattern of writing down every drink before you start it, it becomes easier and more natural.

Situation

Perhaps you've noticed that in certain situations you tend to drink more, whereas in other circumstances you're likely to drink less or not at all. This is no coincidence. The situation around you can strongly influence your drinking, particularly if you're unaware of its influence. Aspects of the situation around you can trigger drinking. Among the things that may influence your alcohol use are:

- The people you're with
- The place where you're drinking
- Being hungry or thirsty
- How much money or alcohol is available
- What you're doing besides drinking
- How you're feeling

Not all of these would be triggers for your drinking, but some may be. How can you find out which factors influence your drinking habits? You could just think it over, but there is a more reliable way.

That's what the "Situation" column is for in record keeping. You could, for example, write down where you are whenever you record a drink. If you do, you might have some entries like those found on the record card on the next page.

If you keep records like these for a few weeks, you may begin to notice patterns. You might observe that you were in certain places when you tended to drink more. You may also find that when you are with

Sample Daily Record Card

Date	Time	Type of drink	Amount	Situation
2/20	7:30	Beer	12 oz.	Lounge—Restaurant Jo
2/20	7:50	Wine	5 oz.	Dinner—Restaurant
2/20	8:15	Wine	5 oz.	Dinner
2/20	9:00	Tequila	Shot	Lounge—Restaurant
2/21	7:00	Beer	12 oz.	Home alone
2/23	6:30	Scotch	~2 oz.	Jay's house Jay, Kris

certain people you drink less. Here's how your daily record cards can help you discover some triggers for your drinking.

1. Start out by recording only one or two factors—for example, whom you're with and where you are.

2. Keep records of every drink you have and make these notes in the "Situation" column of your cards. Try this for 2 weeks or so.

3. Sit down with the records you've kept. Lay them out and look them over, looking particularly for days when you drank more. Were you in certain places or with certain people at those times? Do you see any patterns?

4. As you become accustomed to recording the situation, add another aspect that you think might be important. What are your

hunches about circumstances in which you overdrink? Might it be how you're feeling? What else you're doing? As you continue keeping records, see if your hunches are confirmed.

5. Don't throw your records away. Keep them, at least until you have a clear picture of what may trigger your drinking or overdrinking.

"WHAT IF SOMEONE ASKS ME WHAT I'M DOING?"

Some people are very comfortable writing down their drinks around other people, but others are concerned about how those around them might react to their record keeping. Our experience has been that most people don't even notice the note taking, or they think nothing of it. As moderate drinking and nondrinking have become more common, you may even find that people commend you for rethinking drinking and taking new steps to manage your alcohol use if you've decided that is the right path for you. Your record keeping will be even less noticeable if you keep your records in a small notebook or on an electronic device.

What can you say, though, if somebody does happen to notice and asks what you're doing? There are no answers that work for everybody, but here are a few of the replies people have used:

"I'm trying to cut down, and I'm keeping track of my drinks."

"I'm on a diet, and I'm keeping track of carbs."

"I'm keeping track of expenses."

"It's something I'm doing for myself."

"It's something I'm doing for a class."

"I'm taking notes for the CIA."

Be creative and see what you can think of to say! Usually a short answer is enough and a long explanation is unnecessary.

Another alternative, if you're in a situation in which you don't want to have to answer questions, is to be more subtle. Following are some creative ways that people have managed to keep their records when they didn't want to answer questions.

Send yourself a message on your phone.

Excuse yourself to go to the restroom or make a call and jot down your entry in private.

Leave the table and go to the bar when you make your notes.

Make a notation on your bill, bar tab, or credit card receipt.

Many people find self-monitoring easy and interesting. Most had never really paid that much attention to counting and spacing their drinks or estimating their own BAC level. Remember that it takes only a few seconds to write it down. The important thing is to figure out a way to record each and every drink *at the time,* just before you take the first sip. Otherwise you're compromising on an important self-management method.

SOME PERSONAL EXPERIENCES IN SELF-MONITORING

No technique has produced more comments and stories from our clients than this process of self-monitoring. A few of these experiences may be helpful as you get started with your own record keeping.

One fellow was particularly conscientious about recording every drink just before the first sip, with accountant-like accuracy. The record keeping became so linked to each drink that soon he didn't even have to prompt himself to keep records. He didn't care who asked or who knew what he was doing. He just told them the truth—that he was keeping track of his drinks. One woman he was dating commented, "I do that with what I eat!" and they joked about their record cards all through dinner. He was still drinking quite a bit during his early weeks of self-monitoring, and he observed that, "It's sure good I'm keeping these records, because otherwise I'd have no idea how much I drank." One morning he woke up fuzzy-headed and found he couldn't remember part of the night before. He recalled the first couple of hours, but after that it was a blank. He pulled out his self-monitoring cards, and there they were: drink-by-drink records of the evening, right through his period of memory blackout! He could even estimate the BAC level at which he stopped remembering, which sure enough was just over a BAC of .20.

Another person had trouble keeping her records. She meant to keep them, but something always seemed to get in the way. She didn't have a pen, she left her cards at home, or she just got caught up in conversation and forgot about it. At other times she felt embarrassed or resentful about writing down her drinks. Usually she did try to remember to write them down on a sheet of paper after she got home or the next day, but she found she had trouble remembering exactly what she drank when. After 5 or 6 weeks of this, she was getting discouraged and was ready to give it all up. That's when she had a little flash of realization. "This is so easy, and yet I've been dodging doing it. I'm trying to convince myself that it's just too hard to do, but that's not it. I'm dodging taking an honest look at my drinking." She went back to review why she was rethinking her drinking in the first place, and something just clicked. After that, she said, it was suddenly easy for her to keep records!

A student from the local community college set up a simple record-keeping system on his cell phone, sending a quick note-to-self before each drink. Besides taking classes at night, he worked a full-time job, so his drinking was mostly limited to weekends. Self-monitoring was fairly simple. He rarely drank anything but beer, so before each drink he just sent himself a message that automatically showed the date and time. He was usually with friends in either of two favorite bars that he labeled D or L, the first letter of their names. If his message said only D or L, he knew it was a glass of beer. If he drank anything else, he would also note what it was and the amount. This worked fairly well at first. When they ordered pitchers of beer for the table, he would finish one glass at a time and was careful not to have partial refills. This also helped him space out his drinks, and the recording made him somewhat more conscious of how much he was drinking. The process quickly became automatic, though, and he didn't compile his records after getting home. After a few weeks of this, he sat down one Sunday afternoon to write down day by day what he had recorded. He noticed that his drinking varied a lot. Some days the beers came closer together, particularly early in the evening, and he drank more. Other days there seemed to be more space between beers, and he remembered that on those days he had probably been dancing or playing pool. That's when he decided to start recording what he was doing at the time, and also a simple number rating for how he was feeling right then.

YOUR WEEKLY SUMMARY OF PROGRESS

As we've pointed out, the daily record cards can be valuable in several ways. One of these is that they help you keep track of your progress in managing your drinking. Even small steps toward moderation show up! To really appreciate your progress over a period of weeks, though, you need a way to summarize and interpret your cards. For this purpose, we provide a Summary of Progress form (see the facing page). This form is straightforward. You simply fill in one column every week, making an entry in each of the six lines. We suggest that you begin keeping

Summary of Progress Form

Week ending (date):					
Total number of drinks this week:					
Number of days I stayed within my regular limit:					
Highest number of drinks in any one day this week:					
Number of hours spent drinking on highest day:					
Estimated highest BAC level this week (use BAC table):					

cards on a Monday so that your recording weeks end on Sunday. Make entries on your Summary of Progress Form every Sunday evening. You may copy the form provided here or make your own.

Using the Summary of Progress can do at least two things for you. It will mean, first of all, that you'll be sitting down at least once a week to evaluate your progress. This self-evaluation will be based not on vague recollections (as when you wait until the end of the week to recall your drinking) but on accurate information about your actual drinking pattern. Using the summary form can also provide encouragement. There is no better reward for using self-control methods than to see yourself making progress toward any goal you've set for changing your drinking habits. If your self-management is succeeding, you will see your gradual progress on the cards and on your Summary of Progress.

We recommend that you begin keeping records of every drink as soon as possible. You don't necessarily have to make any changes in your drinking right away. You could keep records for a week or two to get a rough idea of your average drinking rate and to provide a starting point from which to reduce your drinking.

Don't be surprised, though, if the record keeping itself seems to move you toward moderation. Many people find that just keeping records makes them more keenly aware of their drinking. On average, people who began keeping these records reduced their drinking by about one-third in the first week or two, which can be a very good motivational head start.

9

SLOWING DOWN

If you've decided that you want to cut down on your drinking, one of the simplest ways of staying within the limits that you set for yourself is to *slow down* your alcohol consumption. Most people who drink too much do so in part because they finish drinks too quickly. Because it takes a little while for alcohol to exert its effects, they may be feeling the second drink while they're having their third or fourth. Consequently, they become convinced that it takes three or four drinks to get the effect they like. Then, unfortunately, the other drinks take effect. One person told us, "When I feel like I want another drink, I just wait 20 minutes and I feel like I've had one." Think of alcohol as an over-the-counter drug. If you choose to use it, you need to learn which dose produces its beneficial effects and when you are overdosing.

The faster you drink, the higher your BAC will go. Like overeating, overdrinking is often a matter of taking in too much too quickly. Slow down and savor!

Another good reason to slow down is to adjust your tolerance to alcohol. As we explained in Chapter 4, tolerance (being able to "hold your liquor") is usually not a good thing. You need ever larger doses of alcohol to experience the same effect, but your body still has to process it all. As one person observed, "If I could get a six-beer buzz on just three drinks, that would be great. But if I have to drink six beers to get the same buzz that I used to get from three, then I'm at a point of diminishing returns."

Alcohol tolerance adjusts to how much you drink. Even having one drink decreases your response to the next drink. It's that fast. When you drink more, your tolerance increases. As you cut back on drinking, your tolerance decreases.

This chapter suggests some ways of slowing down your drinking, the second step toward moderating your drinking.

TYPES OF DRINKS

People who have problems related to drinking sometimes order and consume *stronger* drinks. By "stronger," we mean that the alcohol content is high. Here are some relatively strong drinks:

- Malt liquor and ale
- Martinis
- Liquor, straight or on the rocks
- Doubles
- Fortified wines: sherry, port, muscatel, vermouth

There's more alcohol in malt liquor than in regular beer; more in port than in a cabernet. All-liquor cocktails such as martinis and Manhattans are more concentrated than those with an alcohol-free mixer, and of course doubles contain more ethanol than singles do. Consequently, if you have these stronger drinks, your BAC will rise much more quickly than if you had been drinking their lighter alcohol counterparts.

One simple but effective way to slow down your alcohol intake, then, is to switch to drinks that are not so strong, that have less alcohol in them. Some *less concentrated beverages* are:

- Mixed drinks (instead of straight liquor)
- Low-alcohol beers—but don't be fooled: "light" beer doesn't necessarily mean it contains less alcohol.
- Table wines (normally about 12% alcohol) instead of fortified wines. Again, check the label. Wine manufacturers are required to tell you the alcohol content.

By selecting less concentrated beverages, you'll be taking in less ethyl alcohol per sip. If you're unfamiliar with these beverages, educate yourself! Experiment with different kinds of drinks. Break out of the habit of "the usual." Browse through a recipe book for mixed drinks, read up on wines, try ordering and buying new and less concentrated or alcohol-free beverages. Nonalcoholic wines, beers, and mocktails are commonplace these days. One way to slow down your drinking is to alternate between alcohol-free beverages and your usual drinks.

Another tip about types of drinks may be helpful. Some drinks are very tasty, and it's easy to drink them fast. These may include blender drinks and sweet fruity beverages such as sangria, punch, mojitos, and tropical cocktails.

There are also plenty of people, however, who overdrink on less concentrated beverages such as beer and table wine. Most likely there are beverages that you tend to drink more quickly than others. Your favorite drinks may fall into this category. Become aware of the drinks you tend to gulp and try some alternatives. Try switching to drinks that have unusual or even less pleasant tastes for you. (Make sure, though, that any unpleasantness is not the sting of concentrated alcohol!)

You may protest, "But I really *like* the taste of my favorite beverages!" Yes, of course you do! It may just be helpful to switch beverages if your goal is to make a change in your drinking. The best way to change your drinking habits is to change your drinking habits. Switching beverages may be most useful if your favorite drinks have a high alcohol concentration. Most Americans who overdrink, though, do so with beer, so it's not just a matter of drinking beverages with less alcohol in them. You may find that you grow to like the beverages to which you switch. Know and enjoy a range of beverages and don't stick to one "favorite." Another possibility is to try alcohol-free beverages that are crafted to taste like your favorite alcoholic drinks. The key here is to use the beverages that make it easiest for you to succeed with the change goals you've set.

MAKING IT LAST

There are some things you can do with any drink, including your favorite, to make it last longer. Basically, these things have to do with sipping.

Try counting the number of sips that it takes for you to finish a drink. Don't attempt to change it at first. Just sip in your normal manner, but keep count. Then try to increase the number of sips you can get out of a drink. This means, of course, you will have to take smaller sips. We recommend you get at least 12 sips (and preferably more) out of each drink. Try it! If you have drinks with ice, try adding more ice about halfway through.

Taking smaller sips won't do you a bit of good if you compensate by sipping faster. It's also important to space your sips. Allow at least a full minute (and preferably more) between sips. If there is a second hand on your watch or on a clock nearby, you can practice spacing out your sips and get the feel of it. Try leaving longer intervals between sips. Don't feel obliged to sip every 60 seconds! What is it like to allow 90 seconds to pass without sipping? Two minutes? When you're first practicing this, you might record the number of sips per drink or how long it takes you to finish each type of drink. Be particularly careful with the first sips of a drink, because that's when people tend to drink the fastest.

One simple trick that helps is to put the drink down and take your hand away from it in between sips. It breaks the habit of holding and sipping. Beware of drinking absentmindedly, which can happen, for example, when watching television. The discipline of slowing down your pace of drinking involves mindful awareness (see Chapter 18), at least at first. You're changing a well-established habit.

SPACING YOUR DRINKS

The basic idea behind drink spacing is to decide that you'll have only one drink within a certain amount of time. This means setting another limit for yourself: a time limit.

As an example, refer back to the occasional BAC limit that you set for yourself in Chapter 7. To stay within this BAC limit, what's the maximum number of drinks that you would consume within *4 hours?*

Write it here: ______ drinks in 4 hours

Now divide this number into 240 (the number of minutes in 4 hours):

240 minutes / ______ drinks = ______ minutes per drink

The answer gives you the number of minutes you would need to allow *per drink* to maintain the occasional BAC limit you have set for yourself. Allow *at least* this much time per drink, especially after your first drink.

Now refer back to your *regular* limit. How many drinks is that for an average day? And how many minutes or hours do you spend drinking on a typical day when you drink?

Write it here in minutes: ______ minutes spent drinking in an average day

Now divide this number of minutes by your regular limit (drinks per average day):

______ minutes ÷ ______ drinks per day = ______ minutes per drink.

This second answer represents the *average* recommended length of time, in minutes, that you would allow per drink.

To summarize the calculations you have just finished:

What is the *shortest* length of time in minutes that you should allow per drink according to these limits? (This is usually the first answer, unless the second answer happens to be smaller.)

Write it here: at least ______ minutes per drink

And what is the *average* amount of time in minutes that you should allow per drink according to these limits? (This is the longer of the two, usually the second answer.)

Write it here: ______ minutes per drink, on the average

Do these time limits seem reasonable? If not, what do you think would be reasonable time limits per drink? If you drank at this rate for

4 hours, what would your BAC be? (Use your BAC table to figure it out.)

The spacing of drinks, or "clock watching," is one of the most commonly used methods for cutting down on alcohol, perhaps because of its simplicity. If you can gradually space your drinks farther apart, you're moving in that direction. Also, if you can stretch out your first drink or two, you have a good head start. For people who overdrink, a common pattern is to have a few drinks in rapid succession. Slowing down the first drink or two sets the pattern for drinking less.

Probably your limits indicate that you need to start spending more time per drink. How can you do this? Here are some suggestions:

1. Make your drinks last longer by sipping more slowly and by taking smaller sips.
2. Allow time to pass between finishing one drink and starting the next.
3. Have an alcohol-free beverage between drinks. (This helps if you feel pressured to order something or if you want to have a drink to hold and sip.)
4. If you like your drink chilled, keep it fresh by adding ice or by keeping it cool (instead of gulping it so that it won't get warm). Wine can be kept cool in an ice bucket, a beer in an insulated can holder.
5. Do something else in between drinks. Have something healthy to eat (and watch out for salty or spicy snacks that make you thirsty). Chew gum. Dance. Talk to someone. Do something you enjoy.

10

ON THE SPOT

Okay, you have chosen sensible limits for yourself (Chapter 7), you're keeping records of each drink (Chapter 8), and you're taking steps to slow down (Chapter 9). What else can you do to stay on track toward any changes you want to make and keep from getting derailed? This chapter describes two more skills you can use on the spot when you're drinking.

SELF-TALK

If you observe yourself carefully when you're trying to make a difficult or even an easier choice, you will find that a silent conversation is going on within you. It happens every day. For example:

> *Should I order dessert? The meal was good, and I already feel kind of full, but it would be nice to have something sweet now. I don't really need it, and I do want to lose some weight. The desserts on the menu look good, though. Maybe I'll wait and see what my friends do, but I ought to decide for myself.*

This all happens so fast that you usually don't pay attention to it, and often there is no need for you to do so.

This is a process that happens, usually silently, when deciding what to do. This internal process becomes more noticeable when you are faced with a new problem or a difficult choice. It's almost as if there were a committee debating inside you. Some members of the committee say "Go for it!" and others aren't so sure: "Now hold on a minute. . . . " You can hear them talking most loudly when there's a tough decision to make.

You may also be conscious of this self-talk when you're learning a new skill. People learning tennis, for example, may silently tell themselves "Now keep your eye on the ball" and "Toss it straight up." New skiers remind themselves, "Bend your knees!" The voice of the coach becomes your own. Talking to yourself silently is natural.

How does this ability fit into managing your drinking? There will be times when you are undecided or confused about what to do in a particular situation. Should I accept the drink I'm being offered? Am I going to have another one? So there you are on the spot, wishing someone were on hand to coach you or suggest what to do in this tricky situation. There's just no one who can do that for you all the time. Or is there?

The fact is that you can do it yourself. For most situations that you face, you probably already have some good ideas about how to handle them effectively. You might even be able to prepare yourself before the situation arises, while there is less pressure to come up with an answer. If nothing else, you can at least reassure yourself and calm down so that you don't make the situation more difficult by feeling overwhelmed. What might you say to a good friend in the same situation? Offer yourself some sound advice as though it were coming from a caring and wise friend. In a way, it's easier to tailor advice for yourself because you know better than anybody else does what you care about and what you're feeling.

What are some of those on-the-spot decisions that you might make about alcohol?

- Choosing whether I will order a drink at a restaurant.
- Remembering and sticking to my chosen limits.
- Taking my time to slow down when drinking.
- Coming up with what to do instead of taking a drink.
- Deciding whether to have a drink when I get home.

What are the different voices on your internal committee, for example, when you're asked whether you would like another glass of beer or wine?

> *I'd like another glass, though I've already had one, and I decided that one a day should be my regular limit. But it couldn't hurt to have another one, just one more. I've been doing pretty well in cutting down, and there's also my "occasional limit" for special occasions. Yet there's nothing special about today. It's okay, though, to have more now and then. It's really up to me. Also, I'm not sure if that glass I finished was really a whole standard drink. Hold on, though; I don't really need another glass. Besides, what they charge for drinks here is ridiculous. I could just have some water or a soda.*

All this might go through your mind in a matter of seconds. What's going on here is called *ambivalence,* and it's perfectly normal.[1] You're considering two different choices, each of which has some points in its favor. You simultaneously want and don't want another drink. You think of a justification on one side, then you think of a reason on the other side of the scale. In between are words such as *but, though, yet, besides,* and *on the other hand.* You're weighing the arguments.

It's often possible to do this decision making in advance before you have to choose. At a bar or restaurant, for example, you can anticipate that the server will come back and ask whether you want another drink, and you can make up your mind ahead of time. You can develop some guidelines in advance, such as "When in doubt, say no."

You know your own arguments pretty well, so you can prepare your counterpoints to them. When you hear familiar reasoning such as "One more drink can't hurt" or "I'm entitled," what are your best counterarguments? They might begin with

- Now just hold on . . .
- You know better than that . . .
- Wait a minute here . . .

You are essentially telling yourself what comes after the *but.* You can decide which members of the inner committee get to speak and who will have the winning argument. After all, it's *your* committee, and you're the chair. You get to decide what to think.

You can also be your own inner coach when you're on the spot, just as people do in sports. Give yourself encouragement or reminder instructions. Here are some examples:

- You can do this—you know how.
- Now slow down and take smaller sips. Put the glass down in between.
- Take a few deep breaths and relax.
- You don't *have* to drink.
- Remember why you set this limit for yourself in the first place.
- Now wait; it *could* hurt, as I know from experience.

You can even practice this in advance. Picture a real situation in which you will be making decisions about drinking. What will the members of your inner committee be saying? What can you tell yourself as a wise and caring coach? Practice and change your self-coaching statements until they feel right. Try this out and learn about yourself! It may be helpful to write down some of your best wise-coach self-statements.

Finally, self-talk can be helpful if you find your motivation to maintain moderation beginning to wane. Again, notice the helpful and harmful thoughts that occur to you. The helpful thoughts are those that come from a caring and wise perspective. Harmful thoughts may come from a resentful, rebellious "I don't care" or "Oh, what's the use?" viewpoint. You don't have to listen to unwise members of the committee even when the voices are loud. You're in charge of the meeting. Call on other members to remind you why what you're doing is important. What are the most persuasive and important reasons for you to reduce your drinking? If you have a hard time remembering them, write them down. You are free, of course, to drink as much as you like, but why have you decided not to do so?

REFUSING DRINKS

Another important skill you can use on the spot when you're trying to develop a habit of drinking less is resisting drinks offered by others. To stay within your goals, it's you, not other people, who should be in charge of whether and what you drink. This means being prepared to decline available drinks. Fortunately, given the social changes we've described, people these days tend to be more respectful of others' choices about alcohol, and overt pressure to drink is less common. Make your own choices and don't have a drink (or another one) just because it's free or because others are doing so.

Often you can avoid unwanted drinks without even saying a word. If someone picks up a bottle or pitcher and moves toward your half-empty glass, just putting your hand over the top or nonverbally waving the person away is usually enough. If you're leaving a table for a few minutes, you can take your nearly empty glass with you. Step away from the table just before a new round is ordered. Order a soft drink. If you find an unwanted drink in front of you, you can just leave it there. In some cultures, in fact, this is how your host knows when you've had enough.

How you verbally refuse drinks will naturally vary depending on who is doing the offering. You would probably say different things to a stranger than you would to an employer. It's up to you to craft some lines to handle situations like this. Here are some that other people have used:

"No, thank you."

"Not right now, thanks."

"No, I'm fine."

"No, thanks. I've had enough."

"No, I just finished one."

"No, thanks. I'm on a diet."

Friends will usually honor statements like these, and that will be the end of it. If someone persists with "Oh, come on!" or "Hey, what's the matter?" just repeat your "No" response firmly. Here are a few possibilities:

"No, really, I'm fine."

"Hey, look—not right now, okay?"

"My doctor told me that I need to take it easy, and I'm cutting down."

"Hey, don't take it personally! I just don't want another one."

or even

"What is it about 'no' that you don't understand?"

It can be useful to practice your refusing skills before you need them. Try out different ways of responding till it feels natural. Make sure that when you do drink, it's your choice and not because of what someone else wants.

Still another way to avoid extra drinks is not to put yourself in difficult situations. Don't go out with a group you know is likely to drink a lot. Leave the party after the first hour. People who make successful changes in their lives often dodge the harder situations at first. Those who quit smoking, for example, often avoid other smokers for a while. Then with time, as they become more comfortable in their new identity, they find it easier to be in more challenging situations without violating their goals.

What if your friends or family usually overdrink? You may find that as you reduce your own drinking, you're out of step with the people around you. If your entire social network has consisted of heavy drinkers, it may seem like a choice between continuing to drink too much and being lonely and isolated. The situation is not really so black and white, however, and there are options. Here are some things that can work:

- Explain what you're doing to some of your close friends and ask for their support. Get together with them in nondrinking situations.
- Strengthen relationships with people who are moderate drinkers

or nondrinkers. Are there people you *used to* enjoy being with apart from drinking? Look them up.

- Try out new groups and activities that don't involve alcohol (see Chapter 14). There are plenty of enjoyable people and pursuits that don't require drinking. Try them out. You're in charge, and no one knows more about your life than you do.

11

DISCOVERING YOUR TRIGGERS

In Chapter 8 we discussed how drinking can be affected by the circumstances in which it occurs. The *Situation* column in self-monitoring can help you become aware of how your alcohol use is being triggered by these external factors. This chapter offers some information about different kinds of triggers, how they can influence drinking, and how you can use that information to stick to your planned goals.

PLACES

Do you tend to drink more or faster in certain surroundings? The particular setting—the room, the lighting, the sounds—becomes subconsciously associated with alcohol. Just as certain situations make it more likely that you'll drink or overdrink, other settings make it less likely.

It may be immediately obvious to you where your trigger places are, but it can also be subtle. It may not be one particular spot so much as places that have certain characteristics. Research has found, for example, that people are more likely to drink heavily in places where the lights are turned down low, certain kinds of music are played, other people are drinking heavily, and competition is high for attractive partners. Conversely, people are likely to drink less when families are around, in well-lighted places, where people go for reasons other than drinking, in restaurants, and where there are activities that compete with drinking.

Suppose you discover one or more places where you tend to drink more than you want. There are several possibilities. One option is to avoid them completely, at least for a while. Give yourself a break from these places. People who successfully reduce their drinking often avoid their trigger situations for a while. The same is true of people who successfully quit smoking. It doesn't necessarily mean you'll never go back. While "on leave" from such places, you might pick up some strategies from this book to help you if you do go back.

If you can't or aren't willing to take a break from these places, you'll have to figure out ways to manage your drinking while you're there. Think of it as walking more carefully when you know you're on ice or a wet floor. Extra caution is called for when you're around your triggers. This is a particularly good time to make careful use of the methods described in Chapters 8, 9, and 10.

Another possibility is to change the situation somehow. If you have a favorite table or seat, move to a new one. Take somebody along with you who will help you stick to your plan. Don't drink "the usual," but try something else. At home you can move the furniture around or change the lighting. If there is a place where you usually sit to drink, sit somewhere else.

If you find through your record keeping that there are other places where you tend to drink less, what is it about these situations that helps you stick to your plan?

PEOPLE

Just as places can affect your drinking, so can the people you're with. Certain companions may make it less or more likely that you'll drink or overdrink. Heavier drinkers, for example, tend to increase the drinking rate of people around them. Obviously, people who push drinks, buy rounds, ridicule moderation, or engage in drinking contests are unhelpful in reducing your use of alcohol.

Sometimes people may affect your drinking through the way you feel when you're around them. In dating situations, anxiety about impressing the other person can contribute to drinking. You may consciously or subconsciously feel a need to keep up with a companion's drinking pace. If family holidays or other gatherings often lead to conflicts, you might drink more than you want to in hopes of staying calm (a tactic that can easily result in the opposite). On the other hand, if someone seems to be trying to control or keep you from drinking, don't give in to a game of hide-and-seek ("I hide my drinking and you try to catch me") or just a rebellious urge to "show them." Or it can be as simple as the fact that with certain companions you just tend to stay out later, prolonging the period of drinking.

Similarly, there are probably others with whom you are likely to drink less or not at all. Perhaps you drink less when you're around people with whom you feel more (or less?) comfortable. How about in a room full of strangers? Is it what you *do* while you're together? If the activities you share are ones with which drinking is usually incompatible (for example, going for a run), then the time you spend together is less likely to involve alcohol. Some people are most likely to overdrink when they are *away from* other people (drinking alone).

Chances are you're already thinking about the people in your life and how they may influence your drinking. A good way to find out how people affect your drinking is to use your daily record cards. Keep track of whom you are with when drinking. You can use initials to save space. After a few weeks of record keeping, examine your cards.

What can you do if you find you drink more than you now want to with certain people? One possibility, again, is to take a vacation from these people, to avoid them for a while. If you think you can't do that, find some ways of bolstering your self-control when you're around them. What is it that causes you to drink more around these individuals?

You may realize that you drink the most with the people with whom you live or spend the most time. Some relationships turn out to be based on drinking together more than you had realized, and changing your drinking routine may even threaten the continuation of a relationship, a friendship, or a business association. It's extra hard to quit smoking when the person you live with continues to smoke. Some companions may feel threatened by your efforts to cut down on drinking because this change in your behavior causes them to think and wonder about their own drinking. These are tough situations, but you do have several options for pursuing your change goals anyway.

1. First, try cutting down your own drinking and see what happens. Sometimes a companion's drinking also decreases. We treated one fellow who always drank with the same four friends, every night, in the same bar. He was open with his friends about what he was doing and why, and one by one they each borrowed his copy of our book and worked on their own drinking. Eventually they stopped getting together to drink. "Don't ever tell that bartender you're the one who wrote that book," he said. "You hurt his business!"

2. Second, ask for support. This requires letting your companion(s) know that you want to reduce your drinking and asking them to help you. You can add that "I'm not saying you have to change anything. I just think it's time for me to cut down, and I'd appreciate your support." Be specific about what you would like them to do (and not do) to help you achieve your goals.

3. Another possibility is to stay in contact but spend your time together in settings and activities that don't involve drinking. The underlying message here might be "I love you, and I want to be with you; I just don't want to spend our time drinking." Or "I really value you as a friend, and I want to spend time together, but I want it to be in places where I'm not so tempted to drink."

4. Then there is the difficult case in which there seems to be no way to be with a particular person without both of you drinking. Here you may be choosing between a relationship and your own health and happiness. It is in this situation that you may choose to take a break from the relationship so as to change your drinking. In the long run the relationship may be lost, but it may also be regained and strengthened. In either event, you've done what you need to do for your own health and well-being.

Whose company makes it easier for you to drink moderately? Some people find they're less likely to overdrink when in a larger group, especially if there is a good mix of men and women (or families) in the group. (Shy people, however, may drink more in larger groups.) Often, being around people of different ages inhibits one's drinking. In general, being around people who do not overdrink and who do not pressure you to drink will make it easier for you to practice moderation. Try to spend more time with the people who make it easier for you and take them along to difficult situations. Revisit relationships that you may have neglected for a while. Try out some new friendships and groups who make it easier for you to avoid overdrinking.

DAYS AND TIMES

People who drink are more likely to do so on certain days or at certain times of the day. Weekends, nights, paydays, holidays, and certain occasions (such as parties, sports on TV, playing cards, or home alone) may be associated with more drinking.

Biological cycles can also affect your drinking. How fast a person's body is able to process alcohol can vary with the time of day. Some people are more likely to drink when they feel tired. Drinking also fluctuates with women's menstrual cycles. The relationship of drinking to these cycles is not consistent across individuals, but it's definitely worth paying attention to as you track your own drinking.

After you've kept self-monitoring records for several weeks, look back over them. Are there certain hours of the day or days of the week when you tend to drink more? Later night hours are often heavier drinking times. People who stay up later tend to drink more, and vice versa. "Morning people" (early to bed and early to rise) are less likely to overdrink than those who come alive when the sun goes down.

One way to constrain drinking is to put time limits on it. Some people decide never to drink before a certain time or after a certain hour. If you restrict your drinking to certain hours, of course, it's important not to speed up your drinking to compensate. Drinking more in a shorter period of time is a recipe for high BAC. Combining hour limits with methods for slowing down your drinking (Chapter 9) can be a winning combination. Drink less per hour and for fewer hours.

Some people drink more on weekends (or days off) than on weekdays. You might say, "Well, of course! On weekdays I have to work the next morning, so I don't drink as much." But that in itself shows that you're already making choices about when and how much to drink. When you consciously decide to drink more on a certain day, it's your decision. Special occasions (such as weddings, holidays, religious and ethnic celebrations) can be particular triggers. All of the dangers mentioned for weekends are there, plus a general atmosphere of celebration. There may be the added incentive of free drinks. Special occasions call for special precautions. Plan how to level off before you reach your regular or absolute limit.

One particular day that can end in overdrinking is payday, especially if it comes right before some days off. The availability of money is usually a factor here, and a few preventive measures may help. Arrange direct deposit of your earnings to your bank or deposit them yourself that day. If you do drink on trigger days such as this, use some additional methods to reduce alcohol such as time limits and slower drinking.

FEELINGS

Finally, certain feelings seem to trigger drinking. Again, this is a very individual matter. Common emotional triggers are feeling stressed, frustrated, angry, or anxious.

As a drug, alcohol may provide temporary escape from feelings and distress. Some people drink when they become nervous or anxious, using alcohol to relax or escape. Some people do find that drinking relaxes them, but there are a few things you should know about alcohol and stress. The actual effects of alcohol on tension are complicated, but it is clear that ethanol is actually a rather poor tension- or anxiety-reducing medication for most people most of the time. Why, then, do so many people say they drink to relax? At best, alcohol sedates you to be less aware of or forget about anxiety or pain for a while, but distress is still waiting there to greet you when your BAC level goes back down. Another reason that people associate drinking with relaxation is actually superstitious. They drink at times when they would be relaxing anyhow and then give the credit to alcohol. For example, some people have a drink after a hard day. As they sit in a comfortable chair in a dimly lit room with the cares of the day behind them, they find they are, in fact, relaxing. When alcohol is used at such times, it becomes associated with relief, and drinking increases. There are also the placebo effects of drinking described in Chapter 4 and the messages in advertising and media that say "I need a drink." Relaxing would probably happen with or without alcohol, and people are less likely to remember their actual feelings as BAC increases. Try sitting in that comfortable chair in that dimly lit room and see if you do relax without drinking. If you do choose to drink to relax, drink slowly, and wait for the effect to reach you. Better still, have a look at the methods in Part Four for ideas about how to feel better without relying on alcohol.

Some people find that alcohol provides temporary release from chronic pain. Although alcohol may alleviate pain, again it's not a very good pain medication, and large doses can create serious problems when used on a regular basis. If your drinking is related to physical pain, consult a pain clinic. Describe your discomfort and explain that you've been using alcohol to relieve it. Indicate that you want to cut down on alcohol use and that you would like to find alternative means for coping with the pain. There are some very good methods to manage pain that don't involve medication.

Other feelings that are often related to overdrinking are sadness, disappointment, and depression. When people experience a major loss such as a death or divorce, drinking can escalate. Some people drink when they feel down, in an attempt to feel better. Disappointments in daily life are also sometimes met with an attempt to drown them in alcohol. Drinking in response to feeling down is more common in women than in men.

The problem here is that alcohol is a terrible choice as an antidepressant. In fact, alcohol has the opposite effect on the body: It is a depressant, a downer drug. Ethanol actually increases depression and does nothing to correct its cause (see Chapter 15). It can create the illusion of helping, though, because people are less likely to remember how they felt after several drinks.

Another common trigger for overdrinking is conflict and related frustration or anger. People sometimes drink after having an argument with a spouse, employer, or friend. Here alcohol is used as a temporary means of escaping from and forgetting the unpleasant feelings, perhaps lingering guilt or anger. A better alternative here is to strengthen your skills for expressing and communicating your feelings (see Chapters 20 and 21).

You may discover that your own drinking is related to these or other feelings. One way of finding out is to keep track of your emotions on your daily record cards or in a separate diary. It's especially useful to write down how you were feeling just before you started drinking. It can be as simple as rating your mood on a numeric scale.

If an emotional experience is triggering overdrinking, there are several general things that you can do:

1. You can make a commitment to yourself not to drink when you feel this way. If, for example, you find that you usually overdrink after having an argument with someone close to you, make it a point never to drink after such an argument. One common bit of advice is not to drink when you feel Hungry, Angry, Lonely, or Tired (remember the mnemonic acronym HALT).

2. This immediately raises the need to have some other way to respond, besides drinking, when you experience your feeling trigger. Just planning not to drink is a plan to do nothing. Rather, plan ahead of time what you could do instead of drinking. That's the purpose of Part Four of this book.

3. Finally, if you're up against an emotional difficulty that just doesn't get better, consider getting some psychological consultation. Drinking almost never fixes emotional problems, and often it makes them worse. There are highly effective treatment methods available for responding to anxiety, depression, anger, and the like.

Part Four

GETTING WHAT YOU WANT WITHOUT EXPECTING ALCOHOL TO GIVE IT TO YOU

12

THE HEALTHY MANAGEMENT OF REALITY

We all live in two worlds—our internal, mental, subjective world, which is only available to each person, and our external, physical, objective world. Together they make up your personal reality. Your internal reality has been under construction since you were born. Your parents and other people in your environment taught you the language you speak, your values, your early goals, even the way you think of yourself. Your external reality was also initially constructed by your caregivers and your neighbors. You learned how to adapt to your environment, how to interact with people, what to eat, whether to exercise, whether to use alcohol, tobacco, or other drugs. As you grew older, you began to take an active role in the continuing shaping of both your internal reality and your external reality. Part Four of this book focuses on ways you can shape your internal reality through your thoughts and shape your external reality through your actions.[1,2]

Many of the strategies you learned when young have worked well for you and for those around you. Those are healthy ways to manage your reality.[3] But sometimes you may have come across strategies that could have negative consequences for your physical health, your emotional health, or your relationships with your family, friends, neighbors, or coworkers. The more alternative ways you have learned to handle specific situations, the more freedom you have to use those that are less likely to harm you or those around you.

Think of it this way: If you know 10 ways to deal with a specific situation and your friend knows only one way to do so, you have a lot more personal freedom than your friend does. You have 10 times as many choices. This part of the book describes many ways to manage your personal reality with the goal of increasing your personal freedom.

Drinking alcohol has been part of human life for thousands of years. It has been used to manage people's day-to-day reality in many ways. It is part of many social events, religious ceremonies, and intimate moments with loved ones. Many people use it when alone, as a pleasant activity, a way to wind down after a busy day, or a way to deal with stress. Both the taste and the physical effects of alcohol can be enjoyable. Some people become connoisseurs and can detect differences in the taste of wine, for example, that most of us are not able to recognize. As we have said earlier in the book, we believe that drinking is a personal choice. But for it to be a real choice, it should not be the only way you have to achieve the effect you are looking for. People sometimes use alcohol to feel more comfortable in social situations or when they are alone and worried or stressed. Learning other ways to handle these emotions and situations results in greater freedom.

HOW TO MANAGE REALITY IN A HEALTHY WAY

How you feel affects how you think and what you do. When you are feeling down, you are likely to have more pessimistic thoughts and behave in less friendly ways. Luckily, the opposite is also true: You can use your thoughts and what you do to affect how you feel.

The healthy management of reality refers to recognizing thoughts and actions that harm your well-being and those that help you feel better about your life and contribute to your well-being. With this awareness you can focus on increasing your helpful thoughts and actions and decreasing the harmful ones.

THREE CHOICES

At any moment, you have three choices. At the present moment, you can think or do something that (1) improves your mood and your life, (2) leaves them as they are, or (3) worsens them.

Once you have made that choice, you again have three choices. You can think or do something that improves your mood and your life, leaves them as they are, or worsens them. If, on the average, you choose helpful thoughts or actions, at the end of the day you will have a healthier mood and a healthier body. If, on the other hand, on the average you engage in thoughts or actions that are harmful to you, at the end of the day you will have a worse mood and a less healthy body.

Unnecessary Suffering

Being human involves some inevitable suffering. You don't always get what you want or need. Sometimes you experience illness or pain. You lose contact with loved ones when they move away or die. These events can be emotionally painful. They involve some level of unavoidable suffering. But sometimes you may add unnecessary emotional pain. For example, you might add negative self-judgment if you don't achieve a certain goal, describing yourself as a loser or stupid if you get a low grade or don't get a job or promotion you were expecting. The disappointment of not meeting your goal is magnified by how you label yourself. A specific negative event (something that happened) is translated into a description of yourself (something that you *are*). The following chapters are intended to reduce unnecessary suffering by describing ways to respond to difficult situations or to get a human need met or a commonly desired enrichment of life without using alcohol to try to get it.

The Inevitability of Risk

There are very few things that you can control completely. Most risks in life cannot be reduced to zero. There are some exceptions, of course. For example, you cannot become addicted to a drug (including alcohol) if you never use the drug. But in general there are no ways of totally eliminating the risk of experiencing difficult situations or traumatic events. The best you can do is to reduce risk as much as possible. The following chapters acknowledge that all people take risks in life, that drinking alcohol involves some degree of risk, and that once you are well informed about what those risks are, you have the right to decide how much alcohol to drink and whether to drink at all.

Alternative Ways of Obtaining the Effects for Which Many People Use Alcohol

Over the years, psychologists have developed ways to manage internal and external reality that help reduce unnecessary suffering and increase the likelihood that you'll enjoy being with others as well as feeling comfortable being alone. Chapters 13–19 describe how you can have a more enjoyable life by handling difficult experiences such as stress, depression, anxiety, insomnia, and a negative self-image. Chapters 20 and 21 focus on skills that make your contacts with other people more enjoyable.

RESOURCES

- Muñoz, R. F. (1996). The healthy management of reality. From Palo Alto University's Institute for International Internet Interventions for Health website: *https://i4health.paloaltou.edu/downloads/HMOR_English.pdf*
- This 2-minute video explains the basic idea: Muñoz, R. F. (2011, January 16). Managing your personal reality [Video]. YouTube. *https://youtu.be/oLQb4S09zh4*

13

KICKING BACK

Among people who drink more heavily, the most commonly stated reason for drinking is to feel good—to relax after a stressful day, as in "I need a drink!" As a central nervous system depressant, alcohol in moderate doses does indeed relax the body to some extent, as do other drugs such as tranquilizers and barbiturates. Unfortunately, nearly all these drugs are addicting and can have undesirable or dangerous side effects when used regularly.

Most people enjoy feeling relaxed. Feelings of tension and anxiety are usually unpleasant, whereas being relaxed is pleasant. This chapter describes several alternative ways to manage your day-to-day reality in terms of lowering your tension level and increasing your experience of relaxation in ways that will not harm your health and well-being.

No one can avoid stress altogether. In fact, you wouldn't want to. Some stress is good for you—the kind that motivates you to fix a problem or that triggers change that produces long-term benefits. Excitement, although it may feel good, can also be stressful. People differ widely in the amount of stress they experience and how they respond to it. If you tend to use alcohol to relax, this chapter can probably be helpful to you by providing additional choices to produce deep feelings of relaxation.

Because of the way the nervous system works, physical tension and psychological tension are connected. The more tense you feel subjectively, the tighter your muscles tend to become. Conversely, the tighter your muscles are, the more tense you feel subjectively. If the muscles relax, psychological tension drops as well. This is one reason people enjoy a massage. Even if you are not feeling particularly tense, relaxing your muscles can produce a very pleasant sensation—a feeling of letting go, of floating, of putting down a heavy load. By relaxing your muscles, you also use less energy and thus are likely to feel less tired at the end of the day. Similarly, if you can relax mentally, your body will tend to relax as well. The mind and body work as a unit. Therefore, learning ways to relax each in turn can give you more than one way to achieve relaxation. By adding these methods to the ones you already know, including the use of alcohol, we hope you will increase your freedom to choose.

Many people do not know how to relax intentionally. This is not an ability that is routinely taught at home or in school—at least not yet. Because this is such a useful skill, psychologists have developed many efficient ways of helping people relax. These methods range from very detailed ways to relax all major muscle groups to using your breath to trigger the relaxation response to using visual images to bring about a feeling of calm. We describe these three in this chapter. These three approaches are based on *doing* something that will produce relaxation. They are intended to actively change what you are feeling, to gain greater control over your current state. There is another path toward achieving a sense of calm that we describe in Chapter 18, which involves becoming purposefully aware of what you are feeling without trying to change anything, without being judgmental about what you are feeling. That path is called *mindfulness* and has been found to have many applications in health care.

In the following section, we describe methods you can use to achieve relaxation. Of course, just reading the instructions won't do a thing for you. Try it! Follow the steps closely. Read all the way through each method before beginning to experiment with it. And then choose which, if any, of these methods feels most useful to you and practice it until it becomes automatically available to you when you decide to relax.

PROGRESSIVE DEEP MUSCLE RELAXATION[1]

When you're ready to begin, choose a quiet room and allow yourself at least 15 minutes of uninterrupted relaxation time. Sit in a comfortable chair. You should not have to use any muscles to support yourself. Let the chair support you. Most people find that closing their eyes helps them focus on each of the muscle groups they will be tensing and relaxing.

The method involves tightening and releasing the main muscle groups throughout your body. First you create tension in the muscle group, making the muscles as tight as possible for about 5 seconds without creating any pain or cramps. Then relax the muscles, letting them become totally loose and letting the tension go completely. Pay close attention to how the muscles feel as they are relaxing, so that you can learn to produce this feeling of relaxation whenever you choose to feel relaxed.

To deepen the physical relaxation even more, you can exhale as you relax the muscles. The relaxed stage should last about 10 to 15 seconds. After tensing and relaxing twice, move on to the next muscle group.

Never tense the muscles in a way that causes pain. The point is to pay attention to how it feels for muscles to tense and then relax, noticing the difference, and to become mindful that you can bring about this feeling of relaxation at will, so that eventually you can relax your muscles without tensing. The goal is for you to be able to relax immediately, anywhere, at any time, even during tense or anxiety-producing situations.

Following is a list of the major muscle groups and descriptions of how best to tense them. Try going through the muscle groups in this order. Remember to tense and relax each group twice. Then move on to the next group of muscles.

1. **Hands.** Tighten your right hand by making a fist and squeezing. Do this twice. Repeat with the left hand.
2. **Forearms and back of hands.** With your right arm resting on the chair and the back of your hand facing up, bend your hand at the wrist, pointing your fingers straight up. Study the tension this creates in the back of your hand and forearm. Repeat. Now do it with the left hand and arm.
3. **Biceps.** Flex the large muscles in your upper arm by trying to touch your right shoulder with your right fist, tightening the biceps. Repeat. Right arm first, then left.
4. **Shoulders.** Bring both of your shoulders up, as if to touch your ears with them. Repeat.
5. **Forehead.** Wrinkle up your forehead by bringing your eyebrows up as far as they will go. Repeat.
6. **Face.** Wrinkle your nose and close your eyes tightly. Repeat.
7. **Lips.** Press your lips tightly together. Repeat.
8. **Tongue.** Push your tongue into the roof of your mouth. Repeat.
9. **Neck.** Press your head against the back of the chair or the wall. Repeat.

10. **Chest.** Take a breath that is so deep you can feel it stretch your chest muscles. Hold it. Release it slowly. Feel yourself relax as the air leaves your lungs. Repeat.
11. **Stomach.** Suck in and tighten your abdomen, as though preparing to receive a punch in the stomach. Repeat.
12. **Back.** Arch your back away from the chair. Repeat.
13. **Legs and thighs.** Lift your legs up from the chair, holding them straight out in the air. Repeat.
14. **Calves.** Point your toes back toward your chest, creating tension in your lower legs. Repeat.
15. **Feet.** Curl your toes downward, as if digging them into sand. Feel the tension in your arches. Repeat.

After you have gone through all the muscle groups and concentrated on the difference between tension and relaxation in each of them, just stay there for a while, enjoying the experience of deep relaxation. Let yourself feel very loose, very light, very much like a deflated balloon: limp and relaxed. Notice how you feel all over your body. Do a mental check of each part of your body, letting go of any tension that remains. If any part of your body seems tense, go back and repeat the tightening–relaxing exercise for that part.

BELLY BREATHING

Another way to enhance relaxation is by using deep breathing, technically called *diaphragmatic breathing*[2] or, more informally, *belly breathing.* At any point in time throughout your day, you can take a few minutes to bring your level of naturally occurring tension down a notch or two. You can do this pretty much anywhere where you can sit or stand without being interrupted. The point is to take a breath that is as deep as possible, that is, that fills the deepest part of your lungs, rather than just the top of your lungs. The way to tell whether you have been successful is to place one hand over the upper part of your chest and your other hand over your belly. As you breathe in, if the hand over your belly moves out, then you are doing diaphragmatic breathing, that is, breathing that uses your diaphragm to bring air all the way to the deepest part of your lungs.

Belly breathing can produce feelings of relaxation very quickly. One of us (R. M.), using a blood pressure cuff, has found that doing just three of these very deep breaths while sitting down reduces his blood pressure readings consistently. So, the feelings of relaxation appear to be accompanied by actual physical changes.

A way to enhance the effect of belly breathing is to use your imagination. For example, imagine that, as each breath leaves your body, the air carries away more and more of the tension in your body and takes you deeper and deeper into a state of relaxation. You can also imagine that as each breath leaves your body, you take a step down a staircase into a deeper and deeper level of pleasant relaxation.

VISUAL IMAGES FOR RELAXING

Another way to relax more deeply is to bring your thoughts into harmony with your physical state. You have relaxed your muscles or used your breathing to relax your mind. You can also relax your mind to further relax your body. Certain visual images may bring your thoughts into balance with your relaxed physical state. These images can be used either by themselves or during your relaxation practice.

1. **Putting down a load.** Imagine yourself carrying all your responsibilities in a big sack on your shoulders. When you begin

relaxing, imagine yourself putting down that sack. During the time you have allotted to relax, you are responsible for nothing. You don't have to *do* anything but relax. You can just enjoy *being*.

2. **The marionette.** This image is particularly good to use while you're tensing and relaxing your muscles. Think of a marionette standing up straight, being held up by taut strings that make it move. If the marionette operator's hands let go of the strings, they will go loose, and the marionette will crumple into a totally relaxed heap. Now: Your brain is the marionette operator and can let go of you whenever it wants to. As you relax each muscle, imagine letting go of the marionette strings, and as your body goes limp, your mind ceases to labor as well and can enjoy relaxing fully.

3. **The balloon.** Imagine yourself as a balloon that has been inflated to full capacity. It is tight, tense. As you use the breathing exercise to help you relax, imagine you're letting air escape from the balloon. As more and more air escapes, the tightness decreases, the tension disappears. You become wonderfully limp and relaxed.

4. **The cloud.** Imagine yourself as a cloud, a calm and fluffy cloud. You are floating pleasantly in the middle of a clear blue sky. Feel the wind touching your face. Feel the warmth of the sun. Feel how light you are. Enjoy the peaceful sensation.

Now stop reading for a while and give these images a try. Find an image that is most relaxing for you. Or come up with your own.

What other images would be relaxing for you? Tailor them to fit you. They might be images of unwinding, letting go, floating, melting, flowing, smoothness, pleasing warmth or coolness, peacefulness, lightness, having nothing to worry about. You might use the image of a particularly beautiful and relaxing place where you have been or would like to go.

PUTTING RELAXATION TECHNIQUES INTO ACTION

Remember, the purpose of these techniques is to help you relax more deeply. If you've been using alcohol to help you relax, practicing deep muscle relaxation as described once or twice a day for 2 weeks will noticeably increase your ability to achieve the relaxed state without alcohol. Then start experimenting achieving relaxation without going through the entire muscle relaxation exercises. Try to reach the deep state of relaxation by tensing only some of your muscles, for example, your hands or your shoulders. Focus on creating the "letting go" feeling that you have been observing as your muscles relax. Use the breathing techniques or relaxing images. How deeply can you relax without the tensing exercises?

When you're able to relax without the tensing exercises, you can use this relaxation almost anywhere. Take a mental inventory of your body tension during the day—perhaps at work or at lunch. Use a mental trigger, such as after a meeting finishes or after each phone call, to remember to check on how relaxed you are and to get to a deeper level of relaxation. This is when the methods become most useful. Even after you can relax on your own, you should go through the whole tensing–relaxing procedure from time to time, just to remind yourself how deep relaxation can be.

Once you can relax without tensing, begin to apply your new skill in daily living. Start with a relatively slow activity. Try relaxing, for example, while reading the paper. Relax as completely as you can without tensing your muscles first. Draw and release some deep breaths. Allow all muscles to relax except for the ones you're using at the moment. Here are some other slow activities in which you can begin:

- Watching television, a movie, or a play
- Sitting at your computer
- Playing cards, chess, checkers, or other table games
- Sitting and talking with others
- Waiting in line
- Riding a bus
- Driving (but don't relax enough to fall asleep!)

Once you can relax during these slower activities, begin relaxing during some more demanding activities, such as:

- Shopping
- Doing housework
- Washing the car
- Having a conversation
- Playing Ping-Pong or pool

Finally, begin using your relaxation skills during the fastest, most demanding activities you can think of:

- Jogging (yes, you can relax while you run; athletes do)
- Running to catch a bus
- Being in a crowded place
- Rushing to finish a project
- Playing tennis, football, or other sports
- Talking to a very angry person
- Taking care of an emergency

It is possible to relax and move rapidly. Athletes and dancers are trained to remain loose as they perform. Doctors in emergency rooms are more effective if they are not too tense. If some of your muscles are too tight, they will prevent other muscles from doing their jobs smoothly. In addition, you will use a lot of energy needlessly. And chronic muscle tension can lead to chronic muscle pain.

There are other ways of achieving bodily relaxation. Some people find that yoga, meditation, tai chi, or massage helps them relax. There are often classes available on these activities. You could find out if there are any in your area and explore what participation would involve.

So, what does all of this have to do with drinking? As we mentioned at the beginning of this chapter, many people drink to relax and feel better, but there are a number of ways to do this besides drinking. If you're skilled in deep muscle relaxation, belly breathing, yoga, meditation, or visual images, you don't need alcohol to relax you. You have other alternatives. You will have the option of using alcohol, but it will no longer be your first or only option.

One final tip relevant to drinking: When people have had a bad experience—a hard day, a harrowing time, a frustration, a scare—they sometimes have a drink. Then the stress begins to decrease, and they think, "Ah, how relaxing alcohol is!" Next time this happens to you, try using one of the methods in this chapter to relax. No matter what you do after a stressful experience, the most likely result is that your tension will start going down. It's automatic, because people just don't maintain high levels of physical or mental stress for very long. If you started knitting immediately after each stressful experience, you would probably find knitting rather relaxing after a while. Let the tension pass first. Use one of these methods to relax on your own. Then decide whether or not you need or want to drink.

RESOURCES

- There are many videos on YouTube that are intended to teach progressive muscle relaxation. One very detailed and easy-to-follow one is this 15-minute video: Connelly, M. (2015, July 23). *Progressive muscle relaxation training* [Video]. YouTube. *www.youtube.com/watch?v=ihO02wUzgkc*

Books

- Benson, H., & Klipper, M. Z. (2000). *The relaxation response* (updated & expanded ed.). William Morrow.
- Davis, M., Eshelman, E. R., & McKay, M. (2019). *The relaxation and stress reduction workbook* (7th ed.). New Harbinger.

14

HAVING FUN

What you do each day shapes both your internal and external realities. The number of pleasant activities you do each day has been found to be related to feelings of depression.[1] To maintain a reasonably happy and balanced life, it's important to do things that you find pleasurable. It's a bit like taking daily vitamins. Having a good number of pleasant events scattered throughout each week is like making sure you have enough to eat and get enough sleep. Perhaps human beings have a "minimum daily requirement" of pleasant and reinforcing activities to remain physically and emotionally healthy. Keeping a good balance of fun and pleasant events in your life is important to maintaining psychological health. Pleasant events can provide pleasurable physical feelings (benefiting your external reality) and thoughts about life being good (benefiting your internal reality).

It's worth noting here that people sometimes equate having fun with drinking. The reason, in part, is that their pleasant times and activities have so often been accompanied by drinking. Some people even say they literally haven't had fun except when drinking. Alcohol is a depressant drug, and thus isn't a particularly good choice for improving mood. (Think about drinking alone, for example.) It's just that alcohol is so often paired in experience (and certainly in advertising) with having a good time. As mentioned earlier, the relaxation and loosening up that occur in social drinking situations also occur when people think they're drinking alcohol even though they're not. An important step in being free to *choose* whether to drink is discovering that pleasure and fun do not require drinking.

What happens if your life becomes short on pleasant events and fun? One common result is a drift toward depression.[2] Ironically, when you become depressed, you feel even less like doing the things you normally find pleasant. The result is a downward spiral. (If you think you're having problems that resemble depression, see Chapter 15.)

Happily, this spiral also works in reverse: When you build pleasurable events into your life, even (and especially) when you don't feel like doing them, your mood tends to improve. This approach has been used successfully as a treatment for depression called *behavioral activation.*[3] You're less likely to feel depressed when you're engaging in pleasant activities regularly. When you get to feeling down, then, in addition to thinking about having a drink, one thing to ask yourself is how many pleasant events you've participated in recently and how many you have planned for the near future.

Pleasant events have both an immediate impact and a long-term impact on how you feel. There are at least three types of activities that have a positive impact on your internal reality:

- Activities that are inherently pleasurable
- Activities that you are really good at and that allow you to feel a sense of mastery
- Activities that you find meaningful, even if they are not inherently pleasurable or that you are not particularly good at, such as visiting a good friend who is ill

At the end of the day, thinking back on activities in these categories that you did that day would provide you with a sense that it was a good day, that your external reality is satisfying. Thinking back on these things at the end of the week will also leave you with a sense that life is good, contributing to a healthy internal reality. Not engaging in any of these types of activities, on the other hand, might leave you with a feeling of boredom, lack of purpose, and a resulting lack of energy.

Pleasant events such as those we just mentioned also have an impact on your physical health. Many pleasant events require that you engage in physical activity, perhaps get some sun, interact with other people; because they use up energy during the day, they make it more likely that you will get a good night's sleep.

So, what can you do if your life is short on pleasant activities that don't require drinking? Because it can sometimes be hard to think of things to do, it's worthwhile to have a plan. Here are some steps:

1. **Make a reasonably long list of those things you like to do.** Some possible categories are:

Things I can do alone:

____

____

____

Things I can do with one or more other people:

____

____

____

Physical activities:

____

____

____

Intellectual activities:

____

____

____

Productive activities:

____

____

____

Meaningful activities:

____

____

____

Activities that I am really good at:

____

____

____

Restful activities:

____

____

____

Things that take only a few seconds:

____

____

____

Things that take a couple of minutes:

____

____

____

Things that require a couple of hours:

____

____

____

Things that take a few days:

____

____

____

Things that don't cost anything:

____

____

____

Things that cost a little:

____

____

____

Things that cost a lot:

____

____

____

Activities at home:

____

____

____

Activities in the city:

____

____

____

Activities in the country:

____

____

____

Make a list of specific things you can do, using these categories to suggest ideas. Be sure they are things that *you* enjoy, or used to enjoy, not just things that are supposed to be pleasant. It's helpful to think of things that you used to enjoy doing but haven't done recently for some reason. Have you stopped going to the theater to see a film in favor of streaming movies alone at home? Given up hikes in the woods? Canceled your subscription to a cooking magazine that used to inspire you to experiment with new cuisines? Quit playing tennis or running? Also consider things that you *might* enjoy—activities about which you've thought at times, "That might be fun." There's one way to find out.

Are you having trouble coming up with ideas? Enter "pleasant events schedule" in an internet browser for hundreds of ideas.

2. **Schedule time to do some of these things.** Planning and scheduling leisure time may seem strange to you, but think of it this way: Having rewarding leisure time is important to your mental health. It keeps you going so that you can function well in other areas of your life. Isn't it just as important to schedule leisure, then, as it is to schedule appointments, a checkup with your doctor or dentist, or regular meetings? Making Friday night "movie night" or arranging to get together with a friend in person or online 1 day a week or even 1 day a month can ensure that you follow up on your intentions to have a good time.

3. **Make sure there's variety in your leisure activities.** Many things that are a lot of fun can lose their pleasure if done too often. This is why it's good to have a long list of possible pleasant activities: It gives you a good menu from which to choose. And doing something too often may be why you stopped pursuing a pastime that was once a favorite. If you tire of one sport, for example, is there another you might enjoy?

4. **Discover the many activities that are popping up that specifically don't involve alcohol.** They include game nights, shows, book clubs, volunteering, active and outdoor activities, learning and creative classes, and wellness and self-care. You can do an online search for "activities in [enter your town's name] that do not involve alcohol."

5. **Remind yourself that it's okay to have fun and that it's possible to have fun without alcohol.** Fun lifts your spirits and helps you function better in other areas of your life. Recreation should be a regular part of your life. If it helps to get more pleasure back into your life, think of it at first as a reward for all the work you do. It won't take long before fun becomes part of your routine as much as going to sleep at night or eating meals.

RESOURCES

- Therapist Aid. (2014, November 4). *CBT technique: Behavioral activation* [Video]. YouTube. *www.youtube.com/watch?v=HBVACtJCN3M.* This is a 4-minute video that provides a simple description of how to use behavior activation ideas.
- The Mayo Clinic has an online set of 12 free lessons on using behavioral activation methods: *https://mccmscontent.mayo.edu/IBH/EMHBA/content/index.html#.* They include several behavioral activation worksheets that can be downloaded for use at home.

Books

- Lewinsohn, P. M., Muñoz, R. F., Youngren, M. A., & Zeiss, A. M. (1992, rev. ed.). *Control your depression.* Fireside Books. This paperback book is intended for lay readers and describes behavioral activation and other cognitive-behavioral methods that you can use on your own. It has a list of 320 pleasant activities and many other forms you can use to set up a program to increase the amount of enjoyment in your life.

15

AVOIDING THE BLUES

Everyone experiences negative moods at times. Sometimes these moods turn into depression. Sometimes it's a matter of being generally "down"—lacking zest and enthusiasm without knowing why. At other times it may be in response to a specific disappointment, loss, or frustration.

Whatever the cause, you begin to slow down. Your energy level is low, and you don't feel like doing anything. If it gets bad enough, you may start to eat less or have trouble sleeping. How can you deal with this common experience?

Unfortunately, "drowning our sorrows" has become such an accepted way of responding to hurt and disappointment that we often brush aside a truth that's undeniable to those who have ever tried it: Alcohol is a depressant drug that is likely to worsen your mood in the long run and often in the short run, too. And it doesn't help to solve the issues that brought on the difficult situation.

To avoid the blues and maintain a healthy mood, it's important to begin by acknowledging that feelings of depression are a normal part of being human. Like feelings of physical pain, they are built into you for a reason: Something is affecting your well-being. Physical pain is a signal that your body is being hurt, and it leads you to try to stop the hurt. Emotional pain, such as depressed mood, is a signal that something in your life needs attention. Most of the time you can do what is needed quickly enough, and you return to your usual healthy mood. Just as when physical pain becomes chronic, negative moods become a problem when they become chronic, too intense, too frequent, and last too long, interfering with your life a lot.

Some years ago, it was believed that serious depression could not be prevented. But now we have clear evidence that at least half of the episodes of depression serious enough to require treatment can be prevented using methods like those described in this chapter.[1–6] And, if depression becomes that serious, we now have many effective psychological as well as medical treatments.

Depression has been found to be associated with substance use. For example, people who experience depression are more likely to smoke, have a more difficult time quitting, and are more likely to relapse after quitting.[7] The same thing may be true of using alcohol.

Some people have used alcohol, tobacco, marijuana, or other drugs to deal with uncomfortable feelings. Perhaps you've turned to alcohol after having an argument, failing at something, or being insulted or rejected. Some people drink when they're feeling down or blue. If you've found yourself drinking more than usual in such situations, could you be using alcohol to manage depression?

The first step in dealing with feelings of depression is to consider whether what you're feeling is a bothersome but common negative mood or whether it might be a serious depression. About 7% of all adults in the United States suffer from a serious depression (called a "major depression") in any one year, and 16% suffer from a serious depression at some time in their lives. Women are almost twice as likely to suffer from such a depression as men.[8,9]

If you've been feeling blue for a while, or if you tend to drink more when depressed, we suggest you fill out the Mood Screener questionnaire available at *https://i4health.paloaltou.edu/downloads/MScreenerEN.pdf* and use the scoring instructions at *https://i4health.paloaltou.edu/downloads/MSandCESDMunoz2005.pdf.* Complete them before reading our explanation of what they mean, so that your scores won't be influenced by our explanation.

The Most Dangerous Symptom of Depression

One great danger from feelings of depression is the possibility that they might lead to suicidal ideas. The combination of depression and drinking can be particularly lethal. If you find yourself contemplating suicide, you should definitely seek professional help. If you feel that you might hurt yourself at any moment, in the United States call 911 or 988 (the Suicide and Crisis Lifeline). Veterans can press "1" after dialing 988 to connect directly to the Veterans Crisis Lifeline. Elsewhere try *www.befrienders.org*, call your local suicide prevention hotline, or go to the nearest emergency service for help. When people are seriously depressed, it is sometimes easy to convince themselves that suicide makes sense. Once the depression is over, people cannot imagine how they could have convinced themselves of that. Only those who make it through a suicidal period get the chance to see how mistaken they were, however, and how bright life can be on the other side of depression. Therefore, the focus during such times must be on obtaining help. Professionals who specialize in suicide prevention remark that people who seriously consider suicide do not really want to die—they want their emotional pain to stop, and they can't think of an alternative. But there are many alternatives now, and even serious depression can be addressed with professional help.

WAYS OF THINKING ABOUT THE CONNECTION BETWEEN DRINKING, MOOD, AND DEPRESSION

All human beings need to learn how to regulate their own mood states as they develop.[10] Some have learned to do so better than others. If you began using alcohol (or tobacco or another psychoactive substance) when you were a teenager, you may have learned to use it to deal with many of the new situations encountered during adolescence. That means that, as you reduce your use of alcohol to manage your mood, you may need to learn new ways to keep your mood within a healthy range.

Although people often drink when they feel down or depressed, again, alcohol actually makes matters worse. Because alcohol is itself a depressant drug, it tends to perpetuate rather than alleviate depression. Its appeal may lie in the fact that during a period of intoxication you forget your problems ("drowning your sorrows") and generally shut down, but on sobering up you inevitably find the problems are still there and your mood tends to be worse, which in turn may encourage more drinking.

MANAGING YOUR MOOD IN HEALTHY WAYS

1. **If depressive moods are an issue for you, don't set as your goal *never* to experience negative moods again.** A more practical goal is to reduce their frequency, intensity, and duration—that is, how often they occur, how painful they are, and how long they last.

2. **Remember not to get depressed about being depressed.** Don't let depression demoralize you! This can happen if you begin to worry about why you aren't happier and to wonder if there is something wrong with you and if you will ever really get over this depression.

Remember: Negative mood is relatively common. It's a signal that something in your life needs attention. It's unpleasant, but that's a reason to take it seriously, not to resent it.

3. **Remember that the task of learning to manage your moods is not yours alone.** Sometimes people with serious depression tell us they're tired of having to pay attention to their thoughts, their activities, and their contact with people. Why should they have to do this when other people do not? In fact, all people have to learn ways to regulate their moods. Some of these ways are better than others. It's very useful to learn what affects your own moods. Some people learn this more naturally, perhaps because they're exposed to people who do it well. Some actually notice that their moods are problematic early in life and begin to read about how to influence their own moods and to put what they read into practice. Some learn good ways to manage their moods, but, when something major happens, those ways are no longer enough, and they look for additional ways to do so. So, if you feel burdened by the task of paying such close attention to your moods, try to remember that it's a task that everyone must undertake. It's just that you may have to learn to manage your own moods more systematically or later in life than others have. The task is still the same. We all have to learn to manage our moods.

4. **Not all depression can be handled on your own.** If you find yourself experiencing many of the nine symptoms of major depression found in the Mood Screener (such as feeling down for a long time, eating less or much more, or having trouble sleeping because of depression), you should seek help from your primary care physician or a psychologist or another mental health professional who specializes in the treatment of depression. Feeling down can also be related to physical illness. If there are indications that you may be ill, a medical checkup is a wise first step.

There is some evidence that if you have relatives who suffer from depression, you're more likely to experience depression as well. Some people fear that because depression runs in their family, it is genetic, and there is nothing they can do to reduce their risk. In fact, people with genetic or other predispositions to depression may be the ones who most need to learn how to manage their moods. People who are not predisposed to depression are less likely to suffer from negative moods, so they don't need the skills as much. Because depression is influenced by stressful events and the way we've learned to respond to them, learning ways to keep your stress within a manageable range and your mood at a healthy level makes the most sense.

PRACTICAL WAYS TO MANAGE YOUR MOOD

If depression is causing you pain or life problems, finding practical ways to shorten the amount of time that you feel depressed is a reasonable goal. Psychologists interested in how depression occurs have found that people can learn to think and behave in ways that help them prevent or treat depression. One of the most researched approaches to preventing and treating depression is called *cognitive-behavioral therapy* (CBT for short). *Cognitive* refers to how your thoughts affect your mood. *Behavioral* refers to how what you do affects your mood. In Chapter 14 we described behavioral methods (using your activities to manage your mood). In this chapter, we describe cognitive methods (using your thoughts to manage your moods). Other ways of managing your mood are described in Chapters 16, 18, 19, 20, and 21.

Rethinking Your Thoughts

If you have ever had a really frightening nightmare, you know that your mind is able to create extremely detailed stories that can have a strong impact on your emotions, even when you're asleep. It is not surprising, then, that thoughts and images your mind produces when you're awake can also have an impact on your emotions. In addition to nightmares, you can experience "daymares," that is, thoughts and images in which, while awake, you scare yourself imagining all sorts of fearsome events. This chapter focuses on the role of your thoughts in how you feel and what you do. Some people use alcohol to deal with disturbing thoughts. There are other ways to do so. Learning what these ways are can provide alternatives to drinking.

At least two approaches have been found helpful in learning how to work with thoughts so you can use them to benefit your mental and physical health. One of them, used in CBT, focuses on learning to identify categories of thoughts that are helpful or harmful to your well-being and increasing the helpful ones while reducing the harmful ones. As mentioned in Chapter 13, another approach, used in mindfulness approaches to health, focuses on learning to become aware of your thoughts and allowing them to pass through your consciousness without letting them affect how you feel. The first approach essentially recommends methods to change your thoughts. The second approach does not focus on changing your thoughts but, rather, merely noticing your thoughts without judgment and letting them pass by your awareness without determining how you feel. This chapter describes the cognitive-behavioral approach. Chapter 18 describes the mindfulness approach.

How Thoughts Affect Your Life

The role of thoughts in our lives has been discussed for centuries. The Buddha is quoted as having said, "We are shaped by our thoughts; we become what we think."[11] The Roman emperor Marcus Aurelius wrote, "The soul becomes dyed with the color of its thoughts."[12]

In more recent times, mental health experts have examined how our thoughts can lead to mental, emotional, and behavioral problems.

Thoughts are not facts; they do not necessarily reflect reality. In working with our patients, we refer to thoughts as "sentences you tell yourself." Some of these sentences are correct; others are mistaken. Some are necessary, and some are unnecessary. Some give you more energy, and some drain your energy. Some help you react well to difficult times, and some just make you so anxious or depressed that you feel too hopeless and helpless to deal with your problems.

One way of thinking about thoughts is that they are like a river that flows through your mind, what has been called a *stream of consciousness.* Becoming aware of where this stream is taking you gives you the option of redirecting it if it's taking you in a harmful direction.

Types of Thoughts

Cognitive-behavioral prevention and treatment methods help patients learn to recognize specific kinds of thoughts that affect their moods. See if you recognize having any of the following.

- **Constructive versus destructive thoughts.** Constructive thoughts "put you together," such as "What can I learn from this situation?" Destructive thoughts "tear you apart," such as "I can't handle this."
- **Necessary versus unnecessary thoughts.** Necessary thoughts help you do what you have to do, such as "I have to fill up the gas tank." Unnecessary thoughts don't change anything (no matter how much you think), such as "I live in California, and there is going to be an earthquake any second now."
- **Energizing versus draining thoughts.** Energizing thoughts make you feel stronger and more capable, such as "I can bring more good things into my life." Draining thoughts make you feel inadequate,

such as "There are so many things going wrong in my life that there is nothing I can do about them."

This is not a "positive thinking" approach; we are not saying that thinking positively will make everything turn out fine. There are necessary thoughts that may be hard to deal with, but if you don't deal with them you will get into deeper trouble. *To manage reality, you need to face reality.* On the other hand, some unnecessary thoughts may be true but don't lead to helpful action, so you don't need to focus on them.

Albert Ellis, a psychologist and developer of rational emotive behavioral therapy,[13] identified several beliefs that he thought caused unnecessary suffering:

- It is a dire necessity for you to be approved of and loved by almost everyone.
- You should be thoroughly competent at everything.
- It is a catastrophe when things don't go your way.
- You have no ability to control your life and your feelings, because unhappiness is totally due to external circumstances.
- If something is dangerous, you should be continually thinking about it and becoming upset about it.
- If something affected your life in the past, it should do so indefinitely.
- It is catastrophic if perfect solutions to the grim realities of life are not found immediately.

Aaron Beck and colleagues developed a treatment for depression and other problems called *cognitive therapy.*[14] Among the many aspects of this therapy was the identification of several other types of thinking that were often found in people who are depressed. Here are some of them:

- **All-or-nothing thinking.** Thinking in extremes, that is, things are all good or all bad, either perfect or a failure.
- **Negative filter** (ignoring the positive). Remembering and paying attention to only negative events in your day-to-day life.
- **Pessimism.** Believing negative things are more likely to happen and positive things are hardly ever likely to happen.
- **Exaggerating problems** and their possible harm and underestimating your ability to deal with them.
- **Overgeneralization.** Taking one negative characteristic or event and seeing it as part of a never-ending pattern—"she doesn't like me → no one likes me"; "I can't do this well → I can't do anything well."
- **Labeling.** Attaching a negative label to yourself or others rather than focusing on a specific issue, such as labeling yourself "stupid" because you are not good at math or labeling someone "clumsy" because they have dropped something.

Most people have some of these types of thoughts without noticing them. For example, the negative filter pattern is almost universal. As you go about your day, when things go as expected and people treat you well, you hardly notice. But if someone is particularly rude to you, say another person in the supermarket line, you tend to remember that for the rest of the day, sometimes ruminating about the interaction, thinking and thinking about what you "should have said" in response to their rude behavior. You are much more sensitive to things that do not go your way and are more likely to bring them back into your consciousness again and again. Of course, the result is that you relive the negative feelings that surrounded that interaction, even though doing so is unnecessary and harms your mood.

Talking Caringly and Wisely to Yourself

We noted earlier that one successful method in treatment and prevention programs is to focus on the earlier definition of thoughts as "sentences you tell yourself." Patients and participants in prevention programs are taught to ask themselves whether the thoughts they are used to having are more like things they would say to someone they care for or whether those thoughts are the things someone who wants to hurt them would say. For example, when something doesn't go well, which of these would you say to a loved one? "I'm sorry it didn't go well. Are there things you could learn from this that would work better next time?" Or "You are a loser! You can't do anything right! You'll never amount to anything!" Then patients are asked to think back on the way they talk to themselves and whether they could begin to notice when they talk to themselves in hurtful ways and try not to do so as often. Talking to yourself when you're doing something that requires extra attention is very common. For example, when getting ready to go to a party, you might ask yourself "What should I wear? Will most people dress up or go casual?" Or, when you were learning to drive, you might have been telling yourself, "What is the speed limit here? Watch for that cyclist. There are kids on the sidewalk—slow down." Once you get good at driving, you are less likely to be aware that you're giving yourself directions—it becomes more automatic. Because this is something you already do, you might as well learn to talk to yourself in helpful ways.

Talking to Yourself about Drinking

If you're "sober curious" and want to experience going without drinking for a while, you might say something like this to yourself: "I wonder what it will be like to not drink at the party. I'll probably need to have something to drink in my hand, perhaps water or ginger ale or a mocktail. I think I am more likely to be sociable when I drink. Maybe I could hang around the people I am most comfortable with. That will make it easier to join the conversation."

If you will be drinking but want to limit your drinking, you might think: "Remember to take smaller sips and enjoy each sip. Drink slowly. Order nonalcoholic drinks after having that first drink."

In either case, you may also want to prepare what to say when people offer you a drink that you have decided not to have. You may say to yourself: "I don't need to explain why I'm not drinking (or drinking more). Just say 'I'm good, thanks.' "

Constructing Your Internal Reality

You live in your internal reality as much as or more than you live in your external reality. Your thoughts, that is, your mental life, have a major impact on your well-being. You're the only one who lives in that world, who knows what you're thinking (unless you choose to share some of your thoughts with others). Although external events can influence your thinking, ultimately you have the power to shape your internal reality, to sculpt it, to create an internal world that is more caring, that provides you with more energy, strength, and resiliency.

Once you become aware that you spend a good part of your life in your internal reality, you can decide that you will construct the kind of mental world that you want to live in. You will not allow external events, other people, or other sources of ideas to decide how you will think. You will learn to redirect your stream of consciousness so it will take you where you want to go.

In choosing how to construct your internal reality, your mental world, you need to become conscious of what your values and your goals in life are. Your values are the general principles or guidelines you have chosen to live by. Your goals are specific objectives you'd like to accomplish. And, of course, there are also your preferences, the things you find pleasurable, the feelings you want to experience, the things that bring you a sense of contentment and fulfillment, the things that make *your* life worth living. Begin purposefully creating your internal world by choosing thoughts that are compatible with your values, that contribute to reaching your goals, that provide a safe, nurturing, and pleasant mental environment to make your day-to-day life enjoyable, that contribute to a healthy mood, and that, ultimately, give you greater freedom.

RESOURCES

- The Mayo Clinic offers a set of free online modules on managing negative thinking: *https://mccmscontent.mayo.edu/IBH/EMHMT/content/index.html#*

Books

- Burns, D. D. (1999). *Feeling good: The new mood therapy* (rev. and updated ed.). Avon Books.
- Ellis, A., & Harper, R. A. (1975). *A guide to rational living.* Wilshire.
- Greenberger, D., & Padesky, C. A. (2016). *Mind over mood: Change how you feel by changing the way you think* (2nd ed.). Guilford Press.
- Williams, M., Teasdale, J., Segal, Z., & Kabat-Zinn, J. (2025). *The mindful way through depression: Freeing yourself from chronic unhappiness* (2nd ed.). Guilford Press.

16

FEELING GOOD ABOUT YOURSELF

Do you ever blame yourself for a disappointment or "failure" and reach for a drink to escape the sneaking suspicion that *you're* the disappointment or failure? If you tend to think about yourself in a negative way, it's not surprising that you might want to get away from those unpleasant thoughts and feelings of self-doubt. Alcohol, unfortunately, is only a temporary way out, if any way out at all. This chapter describes some ways of building and maintaining a positive self-concept (what you think about yourself) and positive self-esteem (how you feel about yourself) rather than trying to use alcohol to run away from these negative assessments of yourself.

Your self-concept is an important part of your internal reality. It does not exist in the physical world. There is no way to observe it or measure it without asking you to describe it. Only you can change your self-concept or know when it has changed. Changing your self-concept involves shaping your internal reality, your mental world. Therefore, this chapter focuses on ways to mold the part of your internal reality most relevant to how you think about yourself.

Feelings of worthlessness (low self-esteem) are usually enmeshed with harmful thoughts about yourself (self-concept). If most thoughts about yourself are negative, then probably most feelings about yourself are also negative. One way of maintaining a positive self-concept is to increase your helpful self-thoughts and decrease your harmful self-thoughts. An image that can be helpful is to think of your internal environment as being similar in some ways to your external environment. Just as much of the world is now attempting to reduce pollution and to rehabilitate parts of our environment that have become toxic, so too can you identify those thoughts that are toxic to your self-concept and weed them out of your internal world, while planting and caring for those health-engendering thoughts that give you a sense of worth, a feeling of energy, a sense of being a good person. Of course, one way to increase helpful thoughts about yourself is to pay attention to positive things you have done so you can remember them in the future. So, a way to improve your internal (mental) world is to do things in your external (day-to-day) world that you can feel proud of.

INCREASING HELPFUL SELF-THOUGHTS

Thinking helpful thoughts doesn't always come naturally. Here are a couple of ways to make it a habit.

Set Up Reminders for Yourself

Sometimes it helps to have a reminder to think well of yourself. You could stick a piece of tape on the face of your watch, so that each time you check the time you will remember to think a helpful thought. You might put a bit of colored tape on your cell phone or your key ring so that each time you use them you will be reminded. You can probably think of other possibilities that will fit your own lifestyle better.

The general idea is to use something that you do frequently to remind yourself to do something else that you are now doing less often. The effect of this method is even stronger if you practice doing the infrequent thing (in this case, think a helpful thought about yourself) before you perform the more frequent behavior (e.g., using your cell phone or keys).

Prime Yourself

Sometimes it's difficult to come up with helpful self-thoughts spontaneously, especially if you're out of practice. For this reason, it pays to sit down and make a list of positive remarks that apply to you. For example:

1. "I'm a responsible person."
2. "I'm a considerate person."
3. "I like people."
4. "Many people like me."
5. "I've been successful at keeping to my plan this week."
6. "I have dealt with difficult problems before."
7. "I have good taste in clothes."
8. "My family cares for me."
9. "I love my kids."
10. "I'm okay."

Make your own list of positive self-statements—at least 10 things you can say to yourself. Set up a reminder, and every time you see it, tell yourself something positive.

You can also try asking someone who knows and supports you to help you come up with a list of your positive characteristics. Perhaps you could say that you've been reading a book about how to improve your self-concept and the authors suggested you do this with a close friend. You could take turns coming up with positive characteristics you see in each other. Below is a list of positive characteristics of people who succeed with change. Which of these are true of you? Why?

List of Positive Characteristics				
Accepting	Committed	Flexible	Persevering	Stubborn
Active	Competent	Focused	Persistent	Thankful
Adaptable	Concerned	Forgiving	Positive	Thorough
Adventuresome	Confident	Forward-looking	Powerful	Thoughtful
Affectionate	Considerate	Free	Prayerful	Tough
Affirmative	Courageous	Happy	Quick	Trusting
Alert	Creative	Healthy	Reasonable	Trustworthy
Alive	Decisive	Hopeful	Receptive	Truthful
Ambitious	Dedicated	Imaginative	Relaxed	Understanding
Anchored	Determined	Ingenious	Reliable	Unique
Assertive	Die-hard	Intelligent	Resourceful	Unstoppable
Assured	Diligent	Knowledgeable	Responsible	Vigorous
Attentive	Doer	Loving	Sensible	Visionary
Bold	Eager	Mature	Skillful	Whole
Brave	Earnest	Open	Solid	Willing
Bright	Effective	Optimistic	Spiritual	Winning
Capable	Energetic	Orderly	Stable	Wise
Careful	Experienced	Organized	Steady	Worthy
Cheerful	Faithful	Patient	Straight	Zealous
Clever	Fearless	Perceptive	Strong	Zestful

Go ahead—make your list!

My Positive Characteristics

1. ____
2. ____
3. ____
4. ____
5. ____
6. ____
7. ____
8. ____
9. ____
10. ____

If there are positive characteristics you would like to have, but you don't think you can truthfully describe yourself as having them, consider gradually practicing those ways of acting. For example, if you would like to think of yourself as "considerate," begin acting thoughtfully toward others. Note when you do this so that next time you fill out this list you can honestly use that word to describe yourself because you have been behaving considerately.

DECREASING HARMFUL SELF-THOUGHTS

If, as your helpful thoughts are increasing, you find that your harmful self-thoughts are not decreasing, you can deal directly with them too. One simple but surprisingly effective method is to redirect your stream of consciousness by telling yourself, "Thinking this way is hurtful to me. I choose instead to think differently," or "I choose not to go there." And then practice replacing the toxic destructive thoughts with constructive self-statements.

One of our patients came into a counseling session one day with a big grin on his face and said he had come up with a way to remember what he was doing to himself and how to stop it: He had to stop using TNT on himself. He then explained that TNT stood for "Thinking Negative Thoughts."

Harmful self-thoughts are easy enough to recognize. Learn what your own negative thoughts are and become aware of when you start telling yourself such things as:

- "Boy, am I dumb!"
- "Everybody thinks I'm no good."
- "I just don't have what it takes."
- "I'm not very attractive."
- "I could never be as good as ____________."
- "I'm too far gone to fix up my life."
- "My life is ruined beyond repair."
- "It's all my fault."
- "I'm too old to correct my mistakes."
- "I'm hopeless."
- "I'm a loser."
- "I'm an alcoholic, and I'll never change."
- "Nobody could ever love me."
- "I've hurt others so much, I don't deserve to be happy."
- "What's the use?"

Notice that after even just reading this list of harmful thoughts you probably feel just a little more down or anxious. People often do. Imagine what having this type of thought numerous times throughout your day can do to your mood! Now try going back and reading through your list of 10 positive characteristics of yourself. Do you notice a change in how you feel?

If you are not sure that thoughts can have much of an impact on how you feel, try the following experiment: Imagine you are holding a really tart lemon in your hand. You cut it in half and bring it closer and closer to your mouth until you bite into it. Did you notice that you began to produce saliva? There is no lemon, no acidic lemon juice. But just imagining it triggered your salivary glands. Similarly, harmful thoughts trigger neurotransmitters in your brain that produce feelings of depression, anxiety, and so on. By learning to use your thoughts purposefully you can gradually reshape your self-concept and feel better about yourself and your life.

As we discussed earlier, pay attention to whether you could change old patterns so that you no longer think of yourself as having these bad characteristics. For example, if you habitually hurt others, begin to be mindful when you are about to do so and choose an alternative way to respond. After a while it will no longer make sense to label yourself as someone who hurts others. You will have sculpted yourself into someone who does not hurt others.

If you're thinking that you're just the way you are and can't change, consider Carol Dweck's concept of "mindset."[1] She suggests that you can either assume that the way you are now cannot change (a "fixed mindset") or that you can continually develop new skills (a "growth mindset"). Growth mindsets can help you learn from setbacks, continue to work on goals that are important to you, figure out a different path toward your objectives, and reduce the likelihood that you will consider yourself a failure because you have not accomplished something yet.

Setting Standards for Yourself

The standards that you set for yourself can also affect your self-concept. If you have established standards that are unrealistically high, you're inviting an unending series of disappointments. The more disappointed you become with yourself, the lower your self-esteem.

Unfortunately, there is no easy way to describe what are realistic standards. Of course, it is possible to set standards that are too low. It has been said that if you're hitting the target every time, you're too close to the target. One possible guideline would be to set your standards high enough so that you need to exert a healthy effort to achieve them but not so high that they are constantly beyond your reach.

Setting standards, by the way, is not limited to work situations. You set standards for yourself in many areas, sometimes without being aware of doing so. These areas may include your home, work, education, social life, spiritual life, sex life, physical condition, and leisure activities.

If your high standards include long-range goals, you can break them down into smaller steps. Gradual change that takes moderate, sustained effort is often easier to maintain than dramatic change that takes "all you've got" or more. It is hard to maintain an all-out effort for very long. If, for example, you have a standard (goal) for yourself to be 50 pounds lighter and tell yourself you can't be happy until you've reached that goal, you'll be unhappy for a long time. If you adjust your standards so that every step in the right direction makes you happy, you're likely to feel better sooner. You're also more likely to reach your eventual goal. For example, if you set a goal of reducing your weight at the rate of 1 pound per week, you will be more likely to succeed. In a year, you will have reached your overall objective, and you will be more likely to keep your weight steady.

Although we can't give you clear guidelines for deciding on realistic standards for yourself, we can point to danger signs that may mean you've set your sights too high. If you notice that you're constantly failing to reach goals you set for yourself and that unpleasant feelings result, reexamine your personal standards. Negative emotional reactions are natural when you're disappointed. They become dangerous when they happen again and again and begin to produce effects such as depression, sleep loss, marked weight loss or weight gain, relationship difficulties, violent behavior, physical symptoms, or overdrinking.

A pole vaulter charges down the practice track, launches into the air, and fails to clear the bar, bringing it down into the sawdust. There are two ways of looking at it: The vaulter wasn't good enough. Or the bar was a little too high.

On Perfectionism

A common source of low self-concept is perfectionism. More specifically, it's the belief that if you're not perfect, you're a failure. This belief can have substantial impact on both internal and external realities. It can be a source of significant emotional pain, and it can also keep you from realizing your potential. If you're afraid of not doing things perfectly, you may not do them at all. The well-known saying "Don't let the perfect be the enemy of the good" suggests that perfectionism can get in the way of doing some very good things. Sydney Smith said it well: "It is the greatest of all mistakes, to do nothing because you can only do little."[2]

This does not mean that you shouldn't try to be your best or to improve on what you've done before. Perfection is unattainable, but it can be a useful guiding star. In past centuries those who sailed the seas using guiding stars never expected to reach those stars. The stars gave them a direction, not a destination.

Of course, none of us is capable of attaining everything we wish for. It's important to be as kind with ourselves when we experience a disappointment as we would be with someone we care for. The concept of self-compassion is relevant here.[3] Just as we would not want to be judgmental when a loved one fails at something, so we ought to be gentle with ourselves in a similar situation. Disappointments are part of human life, not something that happens to you alone. Therefore, being harsh toward yourself when something does not go as planned is unnecessary and usually makes things worse. Accepting your imperfections without exaggerating them is a way to manage your reality in a healthy way.

One final word from the ancient Greeks may be helpful here. The Greek word *telos* is sometimes translated as "perfect," but it actually refers to the natural, mature end state. An oak tree is the telos of a particular acorn. No two oak trees are exactly alike, but each can be perfect in this sense—the natural, fully developed tree that was waiting in the acorn.

Consider this saying (attributed to Shunryu Suzuki): "You are perfect the way you are . . . and you could use a little improvement."

RESOURCES

- For a 10-minute video by Dr. Carol Dweck on mindset, see: Dweck, C. (2014, December). The power of believing that you can improve [Video]. TED Conferences. *www.ted.com/talks/carol_dweck_the_power_of_believing_that_you_can_improve*

  To learn more, see her book: Dweck, C. S. (2016). *Mindset: The new psychology of success.* Ballantine Books.

- A 19-minute video on self-compassion by Dr. Kristin Neff is available at: Neff, K. (2013, February). The space between self-esteem and self-compassion [Video]. TEDxCentennialParkWomen. *www.youtube.com/watch?v=IvtZBUSplr4*

  To learn more, see her book: Neff, K. (2011). *Self-compassion: The proven power of being kind to yourself.* William Morrow.

- Gilbert, P. (2010). *The compassionate mind: A new approach to life's challenges.* New Harbinger.

17

GETTING THE SLEEP YOU NEED

When was the last time you slept "like a baby"? Probably about the time you emerged from infancy. What was once a natural ability seems to elude many adults. In fact about 19.5% of women and 14% of men are troubled by insomnia[1]—problems with getting to sleep or staying asleep. Among people with alcohol use disorders, the percentage is even higher, both while drinking and during recovery.[2] You don't have to have an alcohol use disorder, of course, to have insomnia, although it is a fact that the very measure many people take to help them fall asleep—drinking—can actually contribute to problems with staying asleep. So learning ways to improve your sleep without alcohol is a valuable goal.

Insomnia has many different causes. Sometimes it results from a specific medical problem. It can be related to depression or to stress. When alcohol is involved, the picture becomes even more complicated. Some people believe they need to drink to fall asleep, yet drinking may well be contributing to the sleep disturbance—a vicious cycle that can make you miserable.

Think about it: Given that there are 24 hours in a day, if you sleep 6 hours a night, you are spending a quarter of your life sleeping. If you sleep 8 hours a night, you are spending a third of your life sleeping. If the experience of sleep is frustrating, if your sleep is not restful, if you toss and turn because you can't sleep, then a good chunk of your life and personal reality is unpleasant at best. We don't blame you for trying alcohol as a remedy, but in this chapter we offer you some alternatives that are healthier and don't exacerbate the problem.

If drinking has caused or contributed to problems with sleeping for you, learning to sleep without using alcohol is key. Managing this part of your daily reality can improve your physical and mental health. And eliminating the need for alcohol to sleep is another good step in managing your drinking.

Many people have no trouble getting to sleep. The strategies discussed in this chapter are intended for those who have trouble getting enough sleep or for whom sleep is not restful. If that is true for you, you are likely to find that one or more of these methods is helpful.

ALCOHOL AND SLEEP

Many people find that alcohol seems to help them get to sleep. Indeed, anything that induces relaxation seems to be helpful in falling asleep. The problem is that alcohol's effects don't end there.

Alcohol is a drug that interferes with the normal sleep cycle in complicated ways. If you're sleeping with alcohol in your bloodstream, you may not get enough of the deepest, most restful kind of sleep and thus may wake in the morning feeling unrested. Alcohol also seems to interfere with dreaming, an important part of normal sleep. Alcohol in the bloodstream at least partially suppresses dreaming. As the blood alcohol level decreases, however, there may be a kind of "rebound" of dreaming. Many of our clients have reported intense periods of dreaming or nightmares during early morning, when blood alcohol levels are dropping. Finally, alcohol seems to make it more likely that a person will be restless during sleep and will wake up more frequently during the night. Not everyone who drinks experiences all of these effects, but in general this holds: Although alcohol may help you fall asleep, it tends to cause your sleep to be disturbed and abnormal.

Thus alcohol and other sedating drugs are not good treatments for most kinds of insomnia in the long run. Furthermore, a pattern of drinking to get to sleep can gradually escalate, causing threats to health or other life problems. If you have been using alcohol to help you sleep, we strongly recommend that you seek another way to sleep well.

If you become accustomed or addicted to alcohol and then decrease or stop drinking, you may develop insomnia as a result of withdrawing from alcohol. If you don't understand what's happening, you may be tempted to use alcohol again to get to sleep, but that only prolongs the problem. In our experience this kind of acute insomnia, which begins when a person decreases drinking, often passes within a few weeks and is not reason for great concern (except, of course, that it indicates some physical dependence on alcohol).

GETTING TO SLEEP WHEN YOU WANT TO

For a long time, sleeping medications were the preferred treatment for insomnia, but in 2016 the American College of Physicians officially recommended cognitive-behavioral therapy for insomnia as the first line of treatment, in part because sleep medications can have side effects and pose the risk of dependence.[3] A number of drug-free strategies have been shown to be helpful to people suffering from the common varieties of insomnia.[2,4] We focus primarily on methods to help you fall asleep more quickly, although we briefly discuss nighttime awakening and nightmares as well.

Relaxation

Falling asleep is perfectly natural, not something that you have to will or learn how to do. When you're tired, you naturally fall asleep unless there are obstacles that block this process. Coping with normal insomnia, then, is more a matter of removing obstacles than of learning how to "make yourself" fall asleep.

The relaxation skills described in Chapter 13 can help. Relaxing helps to remove the tensions of the day. Indeed, research indicates that practicing relaxation at bedtime can be helpful to people suffering from insomnia. So one strategy you could try would be going through the tension–relaxation exercises for all the muscle groups before falling asleep. Once you're relaxed physically, you may fall asleep naturally. The goal here is to focus on relaxing your body and your mind, *not* to "make yourself" go to sleep. After completing the exercises, just continue to enjoy the feelings of deep relaxation, feelings that are compatible with sleeping.

Incidentally, practicing relaxation *only* at bedtime may inadvertently teach you to feel sleepy whenever you relax, which you might not want. So start doing the relaxation exercises at other times of day as well, when you're not getting ready to go to sleep.

Developing a Regular Daily Rhythm

Your body works best when you operate on a predictable cycle of activity and rest. If you continually change the times of day when you sleep, your body can't settle into a regular cycle. Another way to improve your sleep, then, is to pick a regular bedtime and waking time and stick to these as much as possible so you synchronize your biological clock. Turn in at about the same time every night and set your alarm for about the same time every morning. You may find not only that it's easier to fall sleep at your regular time, but also that you begin to wake up at the same time each morning even before your alarm rings. This does not rule out the occasional late nights or mornings of sleeping in, but the more regular you can make your sleep time, the better.

Avoiding Stimulation Close to Bedtime

It may also be helpful to schedule your daily activities so that you begin to slow down as bedtime nears. Parents recognize the importance of this tactic with their children: no arousing or stimulating play just before bedtime. This can be an important factor in your own sleep. Try not to spend the hour before bedtime in activities that require intensive planning, that stimulate many thoughts or worries. This is time for winding down. In general, avoid very active exercises close to bedtime. If you smoke or drink coffee or other beverages with caffeine, experiment with eliminating these and other stimulants in the evening.

In the last few years, more and more people have been using digital devices to read or watch movies or other videos. Using screens near or at bedtime can impair sleep duration and sleep quality. This is often discussed in terms of hurting sleep in children and adolescents. But a 2025 article reports that, in a study with more than 120,000 adult participants, those who used screens more frequently 1 hour before sleep had fewer minutes of sleep per week and were more likely to report poor sleep.[5] Our current understanding of why screen use disrupts sleep centers around three possibilities:

- Digital screens emit blue light, which suppresses the production of melatonin, the hormone that signals your brain that it is time to sleep. Some though not all people appear to be sensitive to this blue light, especially if their screens are set to maximum brightness and are close to their eyes.

• What people are watching can be very stimulating. Action-packed movies, gaming apps, or disturbing news stories make it difficult to transition to a restful state.

• It is sometimes hard to stop watching or interacting with interesting content, so we stay awake longer than usual, which means we get less sleep and wind up sleep deprived during the day.

What's a Bed For, Anyway?

A fourth helpful strategy is to avoid using your bed for anything except sleeping and sex. Often people who have trouble getting to sleep will turn on the light and read in bed or will lie and think in bed and plan the next day. Some people eat in bed or watch television through their toes. If you're in this habit, get out of bed and go to another room if possible whenever you want to read or eat or think or plan. You should associate bed with falling asleep. Of course, some people are perfectly able to read or watch television in bed and then quickly fall asleep, and for them it's no problem. But if you suffer from insomnia, try this strategy; it can be very helpful.

Don't Lie There Awake

This strategy is related to the last one: It's not helpful to lie awake in bed "trying" to get to sleep. If you're not falling asleep and you're becoming emotionally upset about it, get up, leave the bedroom, and do something else.

One way to use this strategy is to choose a length of time that seems reasonable for you to get to sleep. Probably this should not be shorter than 10 minutes or longer than 30 minutes. If, after you retire for the night, you have not fallen asleep during this amount of time, get up and out of bed. Go do something else until you feel sleepy. When you start to feel sleepy, go back to bed, practice relaxation, and allow yourself to fall asleep. If you're still not asleep within the "reasonable" time you have chosen, get up again and start over. Some people find it helpful to get completely dressed when they get up, marking the difference between being awake and falling asleep.

There are two other rules when using this strategy. First, set your alarm and get up at the same time each morning, no matter how many times you've been up during the night or how tired you feel. Second, don't allow yourself to nap during the day. Remember that the goal is to establish a regular sleep cycle. Sleeping late or napping will defeat this purpose.

During the first few days of using this strategy, you may find that you're getting up a number of times. This can be frustrating, but so is lying there awake. Usually within a week or so your body's need for a regular sleep cycle will take over, and the strategy will begin to pay off.

Getting It All Together

These five strategies (relaxation, a daily rhythm, avoiding stimulation before bedtime, using bed only for sleeping and sex, and not lying there awake) work best when used together, although they are of some help individually as well. If you want to work on sleeping better, we recommend starting all of these strategies on a selected night (how about tonight?). Choose regular times to go to bed and to awaken in the morning and honor these times. Choose a reasonable amount of time to fall asleep. Practice relaxation when you turn in, remembering that your goal is to become deeply relaxed. Try not to do anything too stimulating close to bedtime. Don't "try hard" to go to sleep. It's more a process of letting go, of allowing sleep to happen. If you're not getting to sleep, get up and do something else for a while. Don't lie awake and don't read, eat, watch television, or play games while lying in bed. Get out of bed, do something else, and return when sleepy. Regardless of these times out of bed, get up at the prescribed time in the morning, and no napping during the day!

NIGHTTIME AWAKENING

Another problem that people can have with sleep is awakening in the middle of the night and not being able to get back to sleep. A few bits of knowledge may help here.

First, know that it's perfectly normal to wake up briefly during the night. The body cycles through several stages of deep and light sleep, and sometimes in light sleep one awakens briefly. This seems to happen more often as people age.

Second, the fact that you've awakened does not mean you'll stay awake. Sometimes when people find themselves awake in the night, they start saying things to themselves like "Oh no! Now I'm awake and I won't be able to go back to sleep again! Nothing I try helps. I'll be a wreck in the morning!" Such intrusive thoughts are upsetting and tend to cause you to wake up further. It's much better to tell yourself something like "Oh, I'm awake. That's natural, and soon I'll be asleep again. Just relax."

Your relaxation skills can also be used at these times, just as you use them in falling asleep initially. Rather than thinking about waking up or focusing your thoughts on something that will arouse you, just relax yourself and let your body help you drift back to sleep. Let go of whatever thoughts enter your mind: There's no need to pursue them or to keep on thinking about them. Just let your thoughts go and continue to relax.

If your thought stream is moving toward worrisome ideas, try redirecting it toward pleasant memories: wonderful vacations, a memorable romantic tryst, pleasant childhood memories. Then the moments you lie awake won't be filled with desperate thoughts like "I HAVE to get back to sleep!" Instead, they'll be a pleasant interlude between a couple of sleep cycles.

People who suffer from insomnia and who have successfully solved this problem recount many other strategies:

Don't drink fluids just before going to bed so you won't have to wake up to go to the bathroom.

Definitely don't drink anything containing caffeine after 2:00 P.M.

Don't drink alcohol within 2 hours of your bedtime.

Don't smoke or use other drugs within 2 hours of your bedtime.

Don't exercise within 3 hours of your bedtime.

If you wake up in the middle of the night, don't have a snack; your body may learn to feel hungry in the middle of the night, and hunger can wake you up.

Make your sleep environment comfortable: reduce noise (use earplugs if necessary) or use something that generates gentle white noise, darken the room (using a sleeping mask can work very well, as can installing blackout curtains), and arrange for a comfortable room temperature.

If it happens that you wake up and are lying awake for more than the reasonable time you have chosen, get out of bed and return to it only when you feel sleepy.

NIGHTMARES

Some people suffer from insomnia because they have regular nightmares that wake them and leave them feeling upset. It can be harder to go back to sleep when you're jolted awake with a pounding heart, rapid breathing, and feeling cold or sweating (or both). People who have this experience night after night can naturally end up wary of falling asleep to begin with and may use alcohol to lull them into sleep.

Good science is accumulating on nightmares, showing that they can be related to tension level. People going to sleep in a state of muscle tension may be more likely to have a nightmare. For this reason people often learn that a drug that induces relaxation (as alcohol does in moderate doses) may make nightmares less likely to occur. But alternative methods, such as relaxation training, can help significantly. One of the treatment strategies that we tried was teaching people the relaxation skills described in Chapter 13. This proved to be just as helpful as a more extensive treatment method.[6] A number of people suffering from frequent and severe nightmares showed substantial or complete improvement after learning relaxation.

By the way, some people who have nightmares are also concerned that the nightmares mean there is something wrong with their mental health. This is rarely the case. Many of the people treated in our nightmare research program had suffered from severe nightmares for many years but showed no abnormal personality patterns or other major psychological problems.

DO YOU NEED ADDITIONAL HELP?

Online self-help tools showing how to use cognitive-behavioral methods to deal with insomnia have been found to be effective.[7] We have included some of them in the Resources section that follows.

Some sleep problems require more extensive treatment and professional attention. If you've tried the strategies mentioned in this chapter or the digital tools we have suggested for a few weeks without improvement in your insomnia, you may want to seek additional help. Many cities now have a hospital or university with a sleep clinic at which specialists treat these common problems. Your local medical center, a university psychology department, or your personal physician may be able to help you locate a qualified specialist.

RESOURCES

- CBT-i Coach is a free app developed by the U.S. Department of Veterans Affairs based on evidence-based cognitive-behavioral therapy for insomnia. It can be used on its own, but it was initially developed to augment therapy with a professional. It's available for both iOS and Android devices. The VA apps are known for using evidence-based methods and have good privacy policies. When using digital tools it is important to check whether they were developed by experts, whether they have been tested for effectiveness and safety, and whether their privacy policies protect your information. You can find a description of the CBT-i Coach app and links to where to download it here: *https://mobile.va.gov/app/cbt-i-coach*
- The Mayo Clinic has free online modules that teach the methods used in CBT for insomnia: *https://mccmscontent.mayo.edu/PatientEducation/PatientLearning/index.html#*
- Two YouTube videos produced by Dr. Gregg Jacobs at Harvard Medical School explain how to work on insomnia by using your thoughts and your behaviors:
    - (*https://youtu.be/q7amXedTasQ?si=Hz_nR-rCgD1FKWkE*)
    - (*https://youtu.be/XXplGH5v1P8?si=SKa8_MgosXLABUpk*)

Books

- Silberman, S. (2009). *The insomnia workbook: A comprehensive guide to getting the sleep you need.* New Harbinger.

18

TUNING IN INSTEAD OF OUT

Sometimes we just want to get away from negative thoughts and uncomfortable emotions. And some of us find that using alcohol helps us do that. The methods discussed in other chapters can also be helpful in changing how you think and how you feel. In this chapter, however, we present a different strategy to deal with disturbing thoughts and emotions, namely becoming keenly aware of them and learning not to let them move you. This approach is called *mindfulness,* and it can help you more generally to stay calm and centered.

Mindfulness meditation—think of it as tuning in to your internal experience in a way that truly gives you a break—is intended to produce awareness and equanimity. *Awareness* refers to becoming conscious or mindful of the thoughts, sensations, and feelings that we experience from moment to moment. *Equanimity* refers to maintaining a calm mental state, regardless of whatever is passing through our awareness. Learning that this is possible is a major milestone in many people's lives.

Unlike a cognitive-behavioral approach, which focuses on increasing helpful and decreasing harmful thoughts (Chapter 15), mindfulness approaches focus on becoming aware of our thoughts without judging them. Rather than trying to *change* the direction of your stream of consciousness, the image that is often used is that of stepping out of the stream and sitting on the bank of the river to observe your thoughts, sensations, and feelings as they float by. As you see these mental events passing by, you remind yourself that a thought is just a thought, it is just a sentence you tell yourself: It does not necessarily reflect reality, it may or may not be true, and it definitely does not define you or your life. This realization leads you to develop a different relationship with your thoughts and other subjective experiences, which eventually allows you to remain calm, undisturbed by what were once overpowering emotions, pain, and other troubling experiences.

Awareness is described as an ability that all people can use. Awareness is compared with the sky, which has an infinite capacity to hold all the clouds, storms, even hurricanes and tornadoes, without ever being filled completely. Similarly, awareness can hold, without judgment, all your experiences. Becoming mindful of this leads to your ability to face any life event with equanimity.

THE BENEFITS OF LIVING MINDFULLY

Mindfulness training programs have become very popular recently as methods to improve well-being or deal with troublesome physical or emotional conditions. Studies show that mindfulness meditation produces many changes in brain wave activity, cerebral blood flow, and release of neurotransmitters.[1] These changes can affect four core aspects of well-being: awareness, connection, insight, and purpose.[2] The result is an improvement in your ability to be attentive to internal and external reality, increased caring interactions, improved understanding of how your thoughts and actions shape your day-to-day experiences, and greater clarity regarding your aims and values and how to actualize them.

The practice of mindfulness meditation has a long history and is usually described as having been developed within a Buddhist tradition. But similar techniques to reach a state of deep internal peace have also been developed in other religious traditions, such as contemplative prayer in Christian tradition. Many people find these methods useful in dealing with life, and, as they are taught currently in the Western world, they are not necessarily connected to any religious practice.

Viktor Frankl is often credited with the following quote, which points out that our power to make choices resides in learning how to respond to life events: "Between stimulus and response there is a space. In that space is our power to choose our response. In our response lies our growth and our freedom." Getting out of automatic pilot can mean freeing yourself from habits like overdrinking or simply being able to choose whether or not to drink without making a big deal out of it.

You can now benefit from a beneficial melding of Western and Eastern thought that has occurred in the last few decades. Ancient meditation practices from Asia demonstrated one effective way to achieve mindfulness, and treatments integrating these practices with Western science, such as mindfulness-based stress reduction (MBSR),[3,4] mindfulness-based cognitive therapy (MBCT),[5] and finally mindfulness-based relapse prevention for addictive behaviors (MBRP),[6,7] have helped many people cope with medical illnesses, pain,[8] anxiety,[9] and substance use. MBCT has been proven effective in reducing recurrences of depression, especially in individuals who have had several episodes.[10] MBCT uses methods from cognitive-behavioral therapy to help people challenge their unhelpful thoughts, along with meditation to help them achieve awareness and equanimity. MBRP also joins cognitive-behavioral therapy with relapse prevention strategies to help people in recovery increase their awareness of triggers and habitual reactions, to create a new relationship with these experiences, and to develop specific skills to use when faced with high-risk situations. These approaches are also invaluable to people who are moderating their drinking and who face situations that might entice them to drink more than they want or to engage in risky behaviors in general. In addition, they help people who are rethinking drinking to consider not drinking as a simple personal choice, rather than an emotionally charged decision.

Awareness

Most people believe they are generally aware of their environment and their own responses to it. If they weren't, how would they manage to cross the street safely, complete errands and chores, and get to work on time? The fact is, many routine tasks are done by autopilot. How often have you found yourself on the other side of the street or back home from going on an errand without any memory of walking or driving? The ability to multitask may seem like a boon to efficiency—what's wrong with planning your presentation for the next sales meeting while you mindlessly fold the laundry?—but it comes at a cost. Recent research has shown that the ability to multitask may be more myth than reality—that we can't really do two things at once without one of them suffering. Things get even worse when we reflexively react to certain emotions and thoughts with harmful behaviors. Overdrinking is a prime example. Feelings of anxiety or depression can lead to reaching for a drink without consciously thinking about it.

If you have chosen moderate drinking, awareness might involve being consciously aware of the following:

- That you are being offered a drink
- Whether you are feeling like accepting the drink or not
- Whether doing so is in accord with the choice you have made as part of your drinking plan
- That you can consciously choose to accept the drink or not

When you increase your awareness of each of these moments, you increase the likelihood that you will reach your goals. Increasing your awareness that emotional discomfort often leads to automatic drinking might give you the space between stimulus and response that would lead to a choice *not* to reach for a beer.

Equanimity

Equanimity is a state of emotional stability, of not being "moved" by automatic emotional responses to events (either positive or negative), of being able to set aside the tendency to judge yourself or others. When you perceive whatever is going on in your internal as well as external reality, equanimity helps you not to be distracted by your attachment to specific goals or by aversion to specific things or events. You can be aware of what is going on without judging it and thus be less likely to react automatically. Your sense of freedom to live your life the way you have chosen becomes stronger. You feel less buffeted by your usual knee-jerk reactions and more able to truly make a conscious choice.

Equanimity is increased through meditation, because in meditating you learn to observe every part of your experience without judging it. As you observe thoughts moving past the window of your mind like floating clouds, for example, you remember that a thought is just a thought. A thought is not reality. Thoughts are created by your own mind, based on what you have learned throughout your life. They are words you tell yourself. You do not have to react to every thought you have, including (and especially) the thoughts that can cause you the most distress and the most pain. Similarly, emotions do not require automatic, active responses. They can be observed in the same way thoughts are. You eventually learn that the fact that you feel anxious or even terrified does not necessarily mean that anything terrible is going to happen to you. Sometimes it just means that you are anxious or terrified. Just becoming aware of that can sometimes help reduce your fear.

Acceptance is a key element in mindfulness meditation. Acceptance means that you are able to see things as they are, with equanimity, rather than with your usual emotional or behavioral reaction (such as getting angry or depressed and looking for a drink). To change a reality that would be good for you to change, you must first face the reality just as it is, without sugarcoating it or making excuses, and without overreacting to it. Only then can you mindfully choose what you will do given the actual circumstances (rather than merely wishing that things were different or being resentful about the way things are).

PRACTICING MINDFULNESS MEDITATION

You can learn to witness the passing of thoughts and desires that ordinarily lead you to drink by suspending judgment of those thoughts and feelings, of situations, and of yourself. You can learn to accept life as it is, without striving to change it and without becoming upset if you don't reach your goals as quickly as you would like—including the goal of moderating your drinking or of no longer using alcohol. Being able to renew your efforts without getting down on yourself can produce lasting change.

Obviously, old habits are hard to break, and the benefits of mindfulness meditation don't arrive overnight. Mindfulness takes practice. Many experts believe the best results come from regular formal meditation practice, preferably following training by a qualified teacher. It's possible, however, to learn mindfulness meditation on your own and to practice it in an informal way throughout the day rather than at scheduled times. The Resources at the end of this chapter can steer you to several good self-help books and digital tools (apps and websites) with additional information and support. Meanwhile, though, there are a few things you can try to give yourself a taste of a new awareness and equanimity.

Mindful Breathing

If there is one experience we pay little attention to, it's breathing. Many mindfulness meditation programs start with helping participants breathe in a mindful way. To get a sense of what this feels like, try this simplified version for a minute right now.

Sit or lie down in a quiet setting, with your eyes closed or focused a few feet in front of you. Allow your breath to flow naturally, in and out, as you turn your attention to the experience of inhaling and exhaling. You can focus not only on the action of breathing but also on the sensory experience: the temperature of the air as it enters or leaves your nostrils, the change in pressure in your chest, the moment at which your lungs turn from inhaling to exhaling. Your mind will drift, and there is nothing wrong with that. In fact, that's the whole point. You become mindfully aware that you've drifted, and then you bring yourself back to focus on your breath without criticizing yourself for having drifted. Try this for 1 to 5 minutes. You may be surprised by what you notice about this simple, automatic act. You will probably also be surprised by the thoughts that float through your mind, distracting your attention from your breath to a number of other concerns. This little exercise can be a revelation about how fleeting your attention and awareness can be.

Practicing the breathing exercise can be valuable to your efforts to avoid being carried away by an impulse to drink. Many experts advocate use of what is called the "3-minute breathing space," in which you respond to a feeling of anxiety or an urge to drink by taking 3 minutes to breathe mindfully—creating a space between stimulus and response in action.

The Body Scan

A common next step in mindfulness meditation practice is an exercise known as the "body scan." The purpose of this practice is to help people become aware of all of their bodily experience. You may have learned to ignore minor aches and pains on the one hand and to quickly scratch every itch on the other. By doing this you lose the ability to be aware of the full richness of your experience in any given moment. Without that expansive awareness, it's difficult to make fully informed choices.

This exercise is somewhat similar to progressive relaxation (Chapter 13), but instead of tensing and releasing the muscles in each body part or *trying* to relax, you simply focus your attention on one body part at a time and, with gentle interest and curiosity, notice all the sensations that arise from it. To get a taste of this practice, try a little of it right now. It's customary to start lying down on a comfortable surface and engaging in the breathing exercise we just described. Then focus on one body part at a time, typically starting with the top of your head and gradually and slowly moving down to your face, your neck, your shoulders, your arms, your chest, your back, your buttocks, your thighs, your lower legs, and finally your feet and toes. Observe all the shifting sensations in each part of your body without judging the sensation before moving to each successive part. Don't avoid unpleasant sensations; just observe them.

Expanding Mindfulness Practice

In practicing mindfulness and building it into your day-to-day routines, try shifting awareness beyond your body. For example, you can focus on the sounds around you, what your eyes can see, your skin feels, or your nose smells, and eventually your own thoughts and emotions. The goal is to merely become aware of all these sensations without trying to change them and without judging them. You might consider each thought or sensation as a bird flying past the open window of your mind or a cloud floating by in the sky. This practice might reduce the impact of such sensations, making it easier to bear them at other times. If you're trying to reduce your drinking, the acute awareness and acceptance you might develop through the body scan could help you tolerate anxiety, shame, pain, or any other discomfort that you've been trying to manage with alcohol. If you've decided not to use alcohol, even for a limited period of time, becoming aware of what that feels like, without judging your decision, can make that choice less daunting.

Eating Meditation

One way to fit mindfulness easily into your day is to practice it when eating. Familiarly known as the "raisin exercise," it's a good way to get started. More complete instructions are available in numerous sources, such as those listed in the Resources, but what the practice amounts to is this: Take a single raisin and, instead of popping it into your mouth, taking a couple of chews, and swallowing without much thought, really experience the raisin with all your senses. You might start by picking up the raisin and noticing how it feels and looks. Take your time and really look at it, touch it, squeeze it gently. Then put it in your mouth and observe how it feels just resting there. Now feel it all over with your tongue. Again, take your time and notice the texture, scent, and taste before you slowly chew and then swallow it. Many people who try this simple exercise discover to their astonishment that this little shriveled dried fruit is nothing like what they had thought of as a raisin before. Mindfulness can help you discover something new in objects and events that you generally take for granted.

Eating mindfully can easily become an informal mindfulness practice. As you sit down to eat at least once a day, pay special attention to the experience of eating. Many people find that their appreciation for the food is so greatly enhanced that they actually eat less. If you have chosen to continue to drink moderately, next time you drink a glass, take a sip purposefully, feel it slip down your throat, place the glass back down on the table, and enjoy the sensation of drinking mindfully. Similarly, you can mindfully drink a nonalcoholic beverage and become aware of its flavors and texture and the enjoyable feelings it triggers.

We hope this chapter makes you curious enough to explore how mindfulness approaches could contribute to the healthy management of your life. Mindfulness meditation is one approach that can provide you with many tools with which to challenge habitual choices, notice triggers, observe your usual response, and freely choose how to respond without much emotional upheaval.

RESOURCES

- *The Healthy Minds Program* free app was developed by Healthy Minds Innovation, founded by Dr. Richard J. Davidson, who has published several articles and books on the impact of mindfulness meditation on the brain. It can be downloaded from *https://hminnovations.org/meditation-app.* It provides several audio meditation guides from 5 to 30 minutes long that can be used as you go about your day. Some are specifically geared to sitting meditation and some to active meditation. You can choose from four speakers for each of the audio files. It is a very practical tool.
- *Mindfulness Coach* is a free app developed by the U.S. Department of Veterans Affairs. See *https://mobile.va.gov/app/mindfulness-coach*

Books

- Goleman, D., & Davidson, R. J. (2017). *Altered traits: Science reveals how meditation changes your mind, brain, and body.* Avery.
- Kabat-Zinn, J. (2016). *Mindfulness for beginners: Reclaiming the present moment and your life.* Sounds True. See also Kabat-Zinn, J. (2022, December 23). 5-minute guided meditation with Jon Kabat-Zinn [Video]. YouTube. *https://youtu.be/7WnZisfYMsE*
- McQuaid, J. R., & Carmona, P. (2004). *Peaceful mind: Using mindfulness and cognitive behavioral psychology to overcome depression.* New Harbinger.
- Williams, M., Teasdale, J., Segal, Z., & Kabat-Zinn, J. (2025). *The mindful way through depression: Freeing yourself from chronic unhappiness* (2nd ed.). Guilford Press. This book includes audio downloads in which the authors provide several excellent mindfulness meditation exercises.

19

QUIETING FEAR

Do you ever feel like you need a drink to:

Be more comfortable in social situations?

Prepare for making a difficult phone call or conversation?

Be able to speak your mind?

Have better sex?

Forget about painful memories or worries?

Are there particular situations that you avoid or fear, such as flying in an airplane or being evaluated or rejected, or that remind you of traumatic events or memories?

As discussed in Chapter 13, alcohol is sometimes used to relieve tension. Many discomforts are more intense than simple tension, described by words such as *anxiety, fear, panic, distress,* and *dread.* Everyone needs a way to cope with such strong feelings, and drinking alcohol sometimes can have a calming effect.

Because alcohol is often available in social situations, it is easy to use it and associate it with feeling less anxious. However, it may be inaccurate to attribute a more comfortable feeling to drinking alcohol. You might feel less anxious merely by remaining in the situation and becoming interested in the interactions with others. Using alcohol as your only way to cope with anxiety and fear is unwise and may produce additional problems. For example, you may drink enough to reduce your inhibitions and say things you would not normally say, or you may drive home while under the influence, placing yourself and others in danger.

If feelings of anxiety or fear are strong enough to interfere a lot with your life or activities, trained behavioral health professionals can help you with anxiety, panic, or posttraumatic stress.[1] If, on the other hand, the anxious feelings are merely uncomfortable, the ideas in this chapter may help you deal with them. Having alternative skills to manage life challenges can render them less daunting. Some skills that are useful for responding to life challenges are discussed throughout Part Four, such as the ability to relax (Chapter 13) or to relate well with others (Chapters 20 and 21).

There are also ways to feel less fearful of potentially stressful situations so that you can handle them more easily. One way is to *desensitize* yourself to particular situations. The process of desensitization can be accomplished through a well-tested and relatively straightforward method, if followed systematically. Next we describe three types of desensitization methods. *Systematic desensitization* focuses on remaining physically relaxed while imagining anxiety-producing situations, *coping desensitization* involves learning to relax after becoming anxious while imagining fearful situations, and *live desensitization* involves learning to relax while actually being in an anxiety-producing situation.

SYSTEMATIC DESENSITIZATION

Systematic desensitization makes use of the relaxation skills described in Chapter 13. Remember that anxiety and fear involve both mental and physical tension. Your muscles tighten up when you anticipate stress or pain. By physically relaxing your muscles, you can short-circuit this anxiety. Relaxation and anxiety are physiologically incompatible; it's difficult to experience them at the same time.

Desensitization adds another element to the relaxation method. This is the concept of a *gradual approach.* When repeatedly faced with a mildly threatening situation, you eventually become used to it and no longer fear it. You have almost certainly experienced this—that something that made you anxious no longer does, such as driving or making a presentation at work or school. Once you no longer experience fear in a formerly fearful situation, you can proceed to a slightly more difficult situation, until you become immune to it, and so on, until a formerly overwhelming situation becomes manageable. Systematic desensitization involves using your relaxation skills in combination with this gradual approach. You present yourself with the difficult situation in gradual steps, while you are calm and deeply relaxed. In this way your physical calm overcomes the small amount of anxiety that you feel while you are still distant from the fearsome situation. As you move closer, step by step, you learn to remain calm until you get to the situation you used to fear. Following are some instructions for desensitizing yourself to a fear-producing situation, then an example. Many people have been able to use this method on their own, but if carefully following these instructions doesn't work for you or causes you to feel more anxious, don't press on. You can always seek professional consultation.

1. Make a list of different parts or versions of the situation that make you feel uncomfortable. Choose specific steps or scenes that you can imagine vividly. Your list should include 10 to 20 scenes. You could write each scene on a separate piece of paper or index card or use a digital device to create your list.

2. Next, arrange the scenes so that the least difficult ones are at the top. To help yourself put them in order, rate each scene on a discomfort

scale from 0 to 100, on which 0 means the scene creates no discomfort and 100 means you are very uncomfortable even thinking about it. Ideally your scenes should be evenly spaced on this "discomfort scale."

3. Go through the progressive deep muscle relaxation procedure as described in Chapter 13.

4. Once you are very relaxed, close your eyes and imagine the first (easiest) scene as vividly as possible. Place yourself mentally right in the situation—imagine what you would see, hear, and so forth.

5. If you feel tension building up at all, stop imagining the scene and go back to focusing on muscular relaxation. Your goal is to be able to imagine this easiest scene without any discomfort. When you can picture the scene twice for at least 20 seconds each time without feeling any tension, you are ready to go on to the next scene. This may require three to seven repetitions of the same scene.

6. Take your time and work your way up through scenes that were initially more difficult. Continue imagining one scene at a time until you can vividly imagine it without feeling tension building up. You don't have to go through your list all at once. It may take several practice sessions over time. When you start a new session, begin with the scene you were last able to visualize without feeling any discomfort. Remember, this is not an endurance test. If you feel any discomfort, switch the scene off and go back to relaxing. When you finish a session, be sure to end it with a success—the last scene you picture should be one for which you are totally relaxed.

A Detailed Example

Imagine that you have an important job interview coming up and you know that you tend to be quite nervous in such situations. (Using this method, one of us (W. R. M.), who was nervous about his first serious job interview, not only stayed surprisingly calm but enjoyed the interview and got the job.) Using the preceding systematic desensitization instructions, you might prepare the following sequence of scenes 2 weeks before the actual interview:

Situation	Discomfort score
1. Thinking about the day 1 week before the actual interview	10
2. Thinking about the night before the actual interview	30
3. Imagining breakfast on the day of the interview	40
4. Picturing myself on the way to the interview	45
5. Entering the building	55
6. Sitting in the waiting room	65
7. Being asked to come in	70
8. Being asked the first question	80
9. Being in the middle of the interview	85
10. Making a dumb mistake during the interview	95

You might set aside 20 minutes each weekday to work on this list of scenes. You could find that the first few scenes go by fairly easily, but the higher ones take a bit longer. Make sure you're deeply relaxed before you start to imagine each scene, and stop imagining it if you feel either the queasy feeling in the pit of your stomach that is the first sign of anxiety for you or the desire to pour yourself a drink. Master the last items just 4 days before the interview, and continue to go over them once a day after that. Unlike other times, the night before the interview, do not drink. On the day of the interview you may feel much calmer than you had expected. Imagine that during the actual interview you do make a mistake in explaining a project that you had worked on, but you don't get rattled and are able to correct yourself quickly. The interview goes smoothly, and as you are leaving you realize that, whether or not you get the job, you have presented yourself well. Again, unlike other times, you do not make a beeline for the nearest bar. Instead, you take your spouse out to dinner.

COPING DESENSITIZATION

This variation takes into account the fact that sometimes you cannot get out of fearful situations as easily as you can stop imagining them. It focuses on learning to *cope* with a stressful situation by relaxing away tension. This is done first in your imagination, as a step toward learning to do so in reality.

Here is the variation: Instead of switching off the image when it produces discomfort, maintain the image in your mind's eye. Imagine yourself coping effectively with the situation, and at the same time try to relax away the tension by using your progressive muscle relaxation skills. This is how you might deal with the situation in real life, and this method provides practice in preparation for the real thing. It also helps you identify early feelings of tension and use these feelings as a signal for starting to relax. The gradual approach—starting with the easiest and working up to the most difficult scenes—is still very important.

Every other aspect of the desensitization procedure remains the same. The only difference is that in standard desensitization you are to imagine scenes without starting to feel tension, whereas in coping desensitization you actively reduce tension produced by each scene. Before you advance to a more difficult scene, you should be able to relax away all tension while imagining previous scenes.

LIVE DESENSITIZATION

Either standard or coping desensitization procedures can be applied using the actual objects or situations instead of imagined scenes. When actual situations or objects are used, it is called *live,* or *in vivo,* desensitization.

The difference here is that you arrange a series of real-life situations in order of their difficulty. If you're afraid of heights, you might arrange to look out of windows on the first, second, third, fourth, and fifth floors of a building, or you might arrange to look out of a high window for 30 seconds, 60 seconds, 2 minutes, 5 minutes, and so on. You may be able to use the same scenes that you would use in your imagination.

To use the standard method in live situations, relax deeply and then place yourself in the least distressing situation on your list. If you feel tension mounting, withdraw from the situation and go somewhere to become relaxed again. Once relaxed, return to the scene and repeat the procedure until you can remain in the situation comfortably for a reasonable period of time. (What a reasonable period of time is will vary according to the situation in question.) When you have mastered one situation, go on to the next more difficult one.

To use *coping* desensitization in real-life situations, begin by relaxing yourself as completely as you can. Then place yourself in the least distressing situation on your list. If you begin to feel tense, do not withdraw but rather use your skills to relax away all tension until you feel comfortable once again. When you succeed in this, go on to the next more difficult situation.

EXPOSURE AND RESPONSE PREVENTION THERAPY

Other approaches to anxiety have focused on exposing people who suffer from anxiety to the feared event or object and helping them learn in the situation that the fear passes without triggering negative outcomes. Eventually, the fear is no longer triggered by the event or the object. For relatively moderate anxiety responses, it may be helpful to try this approach, which is a variation of the live desensitization method described in the preceding section. However, if fear becomes too much and you flee the situation, it may actually increase your fear. For severe anxiety, we recommend seeking a therapist who specializes in cognitive-behavioral therapy for anxiety. Exposure and response prevention therapy is one of the methods used by cognitive-behavioral therapists.[2]

SOME TIPS FOR THE USE OF DESENSITIZATION

Each of these variations is better suited to certain kinds of situations. If you're afraid of spiders, for example, it may be difficult to collect enough spiders to do live desensitization. Using your imagination would probably be more practical in this case. On the other hand, the live method might be better for a fear of leaving the house. You could gradually increase your distance from the door or your time away from home.

Once you become familiar with the principles involved, you can combine different versions to suit your situation. For example, you could practice some desensitization items in your imagination, some items using coping desensitization, and some items using live desensitization. Practice the standard method as described at the beginning of the chapter before trying out the variations. And remember: Be systematic!

A final tip on the technique of desensitization: When making your list of distressing scenes, remember that you can vary the discomfort produced by the same object or situation by changing some of its elements, such as size, length of time, distance from you, number of people involved, and so forth. It is very easy to produce any of these changes in your imagination. Use this tip to come up with more evenly spaced scenes (based on each item's discomfort score) for your lists.

DEALING WITH UNPLEASANT MEMORIES

We all have memories that make us wince because they're embarrassing, as well as memories that make us sad or anxious. People who deal with these unpleasant memories by drinking set themselves up to become dependent on alcohol for handling these memories. The old phrase about "drinking to forget" actually fits these people. Unfortunately, until they actually learn to deal with these memories in other ways, the memories will continue to hound them and make them uncomfortable. One way to stop memories from prompting you to drink is to find alternative ways for managing them.

Systematic desensitization can be used to ease painful memories. Arrange parts of the memory in a list, from least to most disturbing element. Desensitize yourself to the list, as explained in the previous sections, until the emotional impact of the memory is brought down to a neutral level. Desensitization can also be an effective way to resolve recurrent nightmares.

If the methods we've described so far don't appeal to you, consider the following alternatives for dealing with unpleasant or unresolved memories.

1. Get it off your chest by telling it to someone you trust. Just hearing yourself talk about it sometimes helps you digest it and work it through. You can ask your friend to just listen, being understanding but not giving any advice or opinion.

2. Write it down. Getting it all down on paper where you can see it as actual written sentences you tell yourself sometimes helps to make the memory more manageable by creating some emotional distance from the memories. Set aside a block of time to do this. Write down the full memory and all that you feel: good feelings, bad feelings, hopes and fears, doubts and certainties. If the memory has to do with a

particular person, you may want to write your thoughts in letter form, deciding later whether to mail it. The value is usually in the writing.

3. Set aside some short times just to think about the memory. During this reserved time, do nothing but review the memory. Don't distract yourself with work, recreation, eating, or drinking. Just sit and think. During the rest of the day, put the memory away. If the memory intrudes, merely tell yourself: "I will devote time to this memory later in the day." The idea behind this approach is that, by controlling when the memory occurs, you can begin to feel mastery over it, and by repeating your exposure to it, you may diminish its emotional charge.

4. Experiment with "reshaping" the idea. If the way you think about a past event continually brings about emotional pain, you might be able to think about the idea in other ways. It can help to conceive of the idea as though it were a physical object that can be turned over, dismantled, or even discarded. For example, some people who have been mistreated or abused as children blame themselves for those experiences. Repeatedly making it clear in their minds that the adults who mistreated them are the ones responsible for what happened can make the memories less excruciating by reducing their guilt.

A key point in dealing with difficult memories or, more generally, with difficult thoughts is to remember that thoughts are just temporary events in the brain, words you tell yourself. They are not always accurate or even relevant to your current circumstances. It may not be necessary to give them much attention, if any at all. Thoughts are not always faithful reflections of reality. They can be distorted by emotions. For example, you might feel lingering anxiety from an unremembered nightmare and begin thinking of other possible reasons for the feeling, which might make you even more anxious. An example we often use to illustrate this is the child who asks a parent "If there isn't a monster under the bed, why am I so scared?"

Even if thoughts are accurate, they may still be both unnecessary and harmful. If you think of thoughts as objects, in this case mental objects, you can learn to work with them so they don't cause you unnecessary suffering. Ideas, thoughts, or memories can be useful tools and are constant companions in your internal reality. You can bring those that are helpful closer to your awareness and put aside those that drain you. Ask yourself whether specific thoughts pollute your internal environment while other thoughts bring light, life, energy, and health to your mental world. This way of thinking can increase your power over your thoughts and decrease the power they have over your feelings.

RESOURCES

- Kirk, A. (2022, July 12). Systematic desensitization: How it works and what to expect. Verywell Health. *www.verywellhealth.com/systematic-desensitization-5214330*
- Right Choice Recovery NJ. (2025, March 4). Systematic desensitization: Steps, application, examples, efficacy, and limitations. *https://rightchoicerecoverynj.com/addiction/therapy/systematic-desensitization*
- Self-Help Toons. (2020, August 10). Anxiety, systematic desensitization and graded exposure in CBT [Video]. YouTube. *https://youtu.be/Yv6ptSKEotA*

Books

- Bourne, E. J. (2020). *The anxiety and phobia workbook* (7th ed.). New Harbinger.
- Clark, D. A., & Beck, A. T. (2023). *The anxiety and worry workbook: The cognitive behavioral solution* (2nd ed.). Guilford Press.
- Craske, M. G., & Barlow, D. H. (2006). *Mastery of your anxiety and worry: Client workbook.* (2nd ed.). Oxford University Press.

20

FORMING RELATIONSHIPS

Sociability and positive social relationships are important to both physical and mental health.[1] Isolation and loneliness produce health effects as harmful as those from smoking and obesity.[2,3] Some people find that drinking makes socializing easier, whether in meeting potential new friends, mingling and communicating comfortably, dating, or maintaining good relationships. Historically, parties and other occasions for socializing have often involved alcoholic beverages. Today, however, opportunities to meet people and socialize without drinking are more common, and it's possible to build and keep good relationships throughout life without relying on alcohol.

In today's world, where people's mobility can interrupt relationships and various factors can increase isolation (such as remote working), socializing has become both more precious and more difficult. It's good to know that you can develop personal skills to take the four necessary steps in forming new relationships: *finding people, meeting people, getting acquainted,* and *maintaining and deepening a relationship.*

FINDING PEOPLE

If you're not around other people, you can't meet them. How can you find situations in which you can meet and talk with new people? A good general rule for making friends is to *do what you find interesting and do it in the company of other people.* With the internet at hand, it's not difficult to identify a class, club, church, group, or volunteer opportunity in which you can enjoy activity with others rather than doing it alone. You are more interesting to others when involved in things you enjoy and do well, and you're more likely to engage with those who have similar interests.

There is ongoing debate about whether internet platforms improve or detract from interpersonal relationships, but they have certainly made it easier than ever to connect with people who have similar interests via online chat rooms, forums, blogs, message boards, and networking sites, as well as dating apps. You may even feel more comfortable, at first, polishing your communication skills in these outlets rather than in person. A key, of course, is not to let virtual connections replace all in-person relationships. Don't give in to doing everything at home and online. Meeting in person matters.

MEETING PEOPLE

Once you've found some places frequented by like-minded or otherwise interesting people, you can go there, not just online but in person. The more comfortable you feel in a situation, and the more familiar you become with the social customs of a place, the easier it is to interact with others. You can even make yourself useful by greeting newcomers, serving refreshments, or helping with setup or cleanup. If feeling comfortable is a challenge, you can use other skills for relaxing (Chapter

13) or desensitizing (Chapter 19). This is also a good time to practice communication skills described in this and the next chapter.

GETTING ACQUAINTED

Getting to know people better involves seeing them in various situations. You can take the initiative here with some assertiveness (see Chapter 21). Of course, not every acquaintance is likely to become a friend. Spending time with people lets you discover which relationships are most promising and enjoyable.

MAINTAINING AND DEEPENING A RELATIONSHIP

Acquaintances turn into ongoing relationships as you practice skills for maintaining and deepening them. We say more about this in Chapter 21, but here are some beginning guidelines:

Be yourself. Be honest about your feelings. Communicate clearly what you like and don't like. If you pretend to be someone else, you're not giving people a chance to meet and be interested in the real you. The widespread opportunities to socialize online can leave you unaccountable, creating an avatar that isn't entirely real and can't be maintained in relationship over time.

Pay attention to and be curious about the other person. Listen. Be genuinely interested in what they have to say and how they see things. Neglecting to pay attention to someone is called "taking them for granted."

Remember that a good relationship requires investing some time and effort. Set aside time that is devoted to your relationship—for talking, playing, sharing, caring. Better still if these occasions don't involve alcohol, which can interfere with paying attention and remembering. Just as it takes a certain number of pleasant daily activities to maintain your health (Chapter 14), relationships also require a minimum number of activities together to remain healthy.

Don't set unrealistic expectations for yourself, for the other person, or for your relationship. No one else can fulfill all or even most of your needs.

Beyond new relationships, take time to share pleasant events with people who are already in your life. Good relationships that you have developed over the years can offer ongoing support and fulfillment. It's easy to lose touch when you move away from old friends, but now online meeting apps let you "get together" virtually anytime you want. You can schedule regular meetings just to spend time together, talk things over, share memories, and so on. Seeing an old friend's social media posts about a happy occasion (a wedding or graduation) or a sad one (a funeral or other loss) can provide the impetus to reconnect, which can lead to renewing the relationship.

LISTENING WELL

For both beginning and maintaining relationships, there are few skills as important as good listening, giving your time and full attention to understanding another person. It's easy to post or blast back on social media without taking time to make sure you understand what someone is saying. This happens in conversation, too: Listening just long enough to know what point you want to make next can make people feel unheard. Alcohol's effect of tongue-loosening disinhibition can further exacerbate impulsive responding before listening.

Online or in person, good listening in conversations is not just silence but a learnable skill. When listening well, you set aside for the time being all the stuff you know and could say and instead focus fully on really understanding what the other person means and is experiencing. As you develop this skill, you have a valuable gift to offer others, including those you love.

Consider what is happening whenever someone speaks to you. Before they say anything, there is something that they intend to communicate. That is box 1 in the communication process diagram below. Then there is box 2, the words they actually speak and how they say it. Next is box 3, the words that you hear, and finally box 4, what you think they mean. Now, there are three places where this communication can go wrong. First, people don't always say exactly what they mean (Arrow A). Next, you may not accurately hear the words they speak; for example, if it's noisy or you're not paying close attention (Arrow B). Finally, the meaning you attribute to the words that you think you heard may be incorrect (Arrow C). It's a guess, and you may

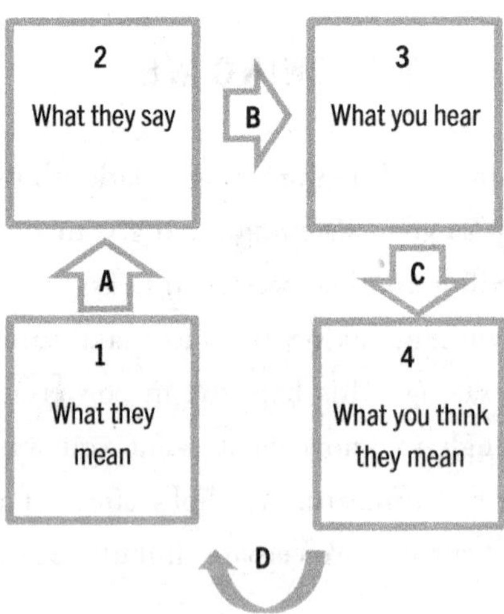

get it wrong. No wonder people are often misunderstood! "I know you think you understand what you thought I said," as people have said, "but I'm not sure you realize that what you heard is not what I meant."

Fortunately there is a skill that you can learn for getting it right. It sounds simple, but actually it's more challenging than it looks and it takes some practice. Basically, it's a way of checking what you *think* the person means (box 4) against what they actually mean (box 1). That's Arrow D connecting the two. You might do that by constantly asking, "Is this what you meant?" but that's awkward and gets old quickly. A better and more skillful way is what's called *active listening.*[4–6] You're making an active guess about what the speaker means, but rather than framing it as a question, you make your guess as a *statement.* Instead of just repeating what they said, you say in your own words what the person *might* mean. Here's a short conversation between a speaker and an active listener.

Speaker: I've been thinking about drinking lately.

Listener: You feel like having a drink. (a statement, a tentative guess)

Speaker: No, I've been reading this book *Sober Curious* and wondering *why* I drink.

Listener: Oh, like what it does for you. (as if continuing the thought)

Speaker: What it does for *any* of us. I do enjoy drinking though.

Listener: So there are some things you like about alcohol. (just restated a bit)

Speaker: Well, that's what I mean. What *does* it do for me?

Listener: Maybe there are some good things and some less good things. (a guess)

Speaker: Right. It's like an investment: What do I get out of drinking for the cost?

Listener: Like what's the bottom line?

All of the listener's offerings are statements, guesses about what the speaker may mean. Even if you guess wrong (as happened first with "You feel like having a drink"), you learn more and get closer to understanding what the person is experiencing. That's the whole purpose of active listening—just to understand better. You're not offering advice, agreement, disagreement, facts, or sympathy. You're listening well.

LEARNING BY OBSERVING

If you feel awkward or shy around people and it keeps you from forming relationships, you could try learning from those who seem to navigate social waters with ease. Do you know people who make communication look easy? Do you have any friends or relatives who seem to be good at meeting and becoming friends with others? Watch them to see what they do around people. It may seem to be effortless, as if they were born with social graces. But that's just because they've learned these social skills well enough to put them into practice quite comfortably. It's a bit like an Olympic athlete who makes astonishing moves look easy.

You can observe and learn from socially skilled people. Try making two different kinds of observations:

1. Observe what they do specifically. You may notice, for example, that people who are "understanding" and "sociable" do things like these:

   Smile from time to time. When do they smile? How much and how often?

   Keep eye contact at a comfortable level. Notice that most

people who are seen as "understanding" often look the other person in the eye when listening. (This can vary greatly across cultures, by the way.)

Show that they are listening. Good listeners show this by nodding, saying "mm-hmm," rephrasing what the speaker said to make sure they understand, offering relevant experiences from their own lives, or showing agreement with comments such as "That's right!" and "I know what you mean" and "I feel the same way sometimes."

2. Also observe the *tone* of the interaction. You may find that people who communicate understanding:

   Maintain attentiveness and seem genuinely interested in the other person

   Show *respect* for the other

   Rarely criticize or complain

   Don't give advice unless asked

   Are not *possessive* or *pushy*

   Pay attention to the other person's feelings

   Match the other's level of seriousness (not making jokes when the other person wants to be serious and not taking things too seriously when the other person is being humorous)

   Help the other person feel at ease

Both kinds of observation are important, and they are related. As you observe the overall tone of the interaction, try to understand just what the person is doing to set that tone. As you discover the skillful behaviors of others, try them out in a way that fits your own style.

RESOURCES

- There are plenty of online resources that discuss meeting people. One example with tips on ways to make new friends is *www.scienceofpeople.*

com/meet-people. The same Science of People website also has helpful information about people skills for forming and strengthening relationships: *www.scienceofpeople.com/social-skills*

- If you prefer reading books, here are two relatively brief ones on listening skills:
  - Miller, W. R. (2018). *Listening well: The art of empathic understanding.* Wipf & Stock.
  - Nichols, M. P., & Straus, M. B. (2021). *The lost art of listening: How learning to listen can improve relationships* (3rd ed.). Guilford Press.

21

KEEPING RELATIONSHIPS

Whether at work, at home, or out in the world, relationships depend on good communication skills. Chapter 20 dipped into good listening so that you can know others, but relationships also involve being known, expressing yourself so that others can appreciate who you are. Relationship is a balance between understanding and being understood.

Do you ever hesitate to express your own opinions or preferences to avoid getting a negative reaction? Or do you find yourself being overly vehement to get what you want or let people know that you mean what you say? Is it hard sometimes to find the right words for expressing what you need and want? If so, join the club. Many people have trouble with expressing themselves effectively, and some do resort to drinking to loosen up or find courage, just as when trying to meet people (Chapter 20). How does that go? Maybe as well as deciding that a few drinks will make you witty and a really good dancer. Fortunately, there are alternatives to alcohol, some skills for effective communication.

I MESSAGES

One such skill is called an *I message* to express clearly what you feel, think, or want.[1,2] The opposite of an I message is a *You message* that tends to blame, shame, or persuade the person. Consciously or not, You messages try to *pressure* someone into agreeing or providing what you want. From being on the receiving end of You messages, you probably already understand that they make it harder to listen and cooperate. They set up a win–lose struggle. The purpose of an I message, in contrast, is to communicate what's going on inside you. It helps the person know and understand you. You may also need to problem-solve or negotiate together, but an I message is a good start.

A first component of an I message is that it begins with the word *I*. When you have a strong feeling or opinion, it can be tempting to start with *You*.

You're not listening to me!

You don't know how hard I work all day.

You don't care about me.

The implicit criticism can shut the other person down so that, ironically, they stop listening. Ideally an I message is clearer.

A second component is a clear expression of what you experience or feel, without intention to blame: *I feel* ________. And a third component makes your experience specific rather than generalized. A simple way to make it more specific is to use the word *when*. Some examples:

I feel unappreciated when you don't acknowledge what I do all day long.

I feel frustrated when I just want you to hear me and you start trying to solve the problem for me.

It doesn't even have to be about something the other person does. Remember that the purpose is to be known and understood:

I am worried about how polarized our country has become in politics.

I feel overwhelmed with everything I need to do.

I'm concerned that my son is drinking too much.

I feel sad when I see homeless people on the street.

Here are two specific tips about an I message. First, make sure it's a *feeling* that you are communicating. People sometimes use the word *feel* to communicate an opinion:

I feel that we're spending too much time on this.

I feel that you're not looking at this objectively.

A clue is the word *that.* If the word *that* logically fits after *feel,* then you're not expressing a feeling. You mean something more like "I believe that ________ and you should agree with me." This is true even if the word *that* is absent but still fits:

I feel we're spending too much time on this.

A second tip is remembering that the purpose of a pure I message is communication, to be understood. It's not a request for a fix, at least not yet. The appropriate response to an I message is to listen well and make sure you understand. If you are requesting a solution, say so after your I message:

I feel frustrated when your papers are all over the kitchen table. Would you be willing to keep your work somewhere else?

I feel lonely when you start trying to fix things right away. I would appreciate it if you just take a few minutes to hear what I'm feeling.

I'm really worried that our sister may be using drugs. What do you think?

BEING ASSERTIVE

I messages accompanied by a request are one example of assertiveness. Being *assertive* means acting in a firm but not overly demanding manner. It means respecting the rights and desires of others, but not to the point of neglecting your own feelings and needs. Being assertive seeks a way for both people to win.

Learning how to be assertive is important for clear communication. Some people insist on their own way and become quite *aggressive* in demanding it, threatening or offending those around them. Other people neglect being assertive and instead remain quite *passive.* Both of these are extremes, often learned while growing up. Assertiveness is a middle way between the two extremes of being too aggressive and too passive.

Aggressive people push too hard. They attempt to get their way by pushing other people around. They may raise their voices, be demanding and unwilling to negotiate, even call the other person names or threaten them. (As you probably know, alcohol lowers inhibitions and increases the tendency to be more aggressive.) The irony is that in the long run this kind of behavior can damage a relationship, resulting in frustration and alienation. By going overboard and being too demanding, you can lose both cooperation and friendship.

Passive people, on the other hand, allow others to determine what's going to happen. They don't express their own feelings and desires and therefore may seldom get what they want. They feel weak or frustrated. Such unaddressed frustration can sometimes lead to drinking to help them feel better or bolder, perhaps leading to aggression. Around and around we go.

Assertiveness involves telling people what you really feel but in a respectful way, particularly when you are saying something that can affect the future. If you're being offered a drink, for example, and you've decided not to drink any more that night, an assertive response would be to tell the person that you don't want the drink. You might say, "No, thank you" or "I'm fine, thanks" or "I'd enjoy another one, but I've decided not to." If the other person insists, you can say "Please don't push; I said no," which is also an assertive response. An aggressive response would be to get angry and snap back. A passive response might be to accept the drink and drink it.

What is considered to be aggressive or assertive varies across cultures and contexts. What might be seen as assertive in one situation or culture may be perceived as aggressive in another.

Some examples of situations that call for some skill in assertiveness are:

- Telling people that you like them or appreciate what they did.
- Speaking up and disapproving of what someone did.
- Asking someone to do a favor for you.
- Telling people when you don't want to do what they have asked.

So of the three styles of communication shown in the table on the next page—passive, assertive, and aggressive—how often do you use each of them? Is there one that you think you may use too often or not enough? How do you think using each of these styles affects your relationships?

Three Styles of Communication

COMMUNICATION STYLE	EXAMPLE	RESPECTS THE NEEDS OF OTHERS?	RESPECTS YOUR OWN NEEDS?
Passive	Hiding or withholding how you feel and think	Yes	No
Assertive	Expressing your thoughts or feelings calmly, honestly, and respectfully	Yes	Yes
Aggressive	Insisting on your own ways or views, demanding, threatening, ordering	No	Yes

Consider times and places at which you could be assertive but instead are too passive or aggressive. You might notice how other people handle these situations well. To practice being assertive, you could start by practicing mentally, that is, in your internal world. Imagine exactly what you might do. Sit down in a quiet place, close your eyes, and start imagining the scene. Imagine the place. Imagine yourself and the other people involved. Then start the action and envision yourself acting assertively. Imitate what the assertive people you've seen might do in this situation. Change their words and gestures so that you're comfortable, but don't lose the assertive quality in them. Be very specific in picturing yourself being assertive. Instruct yourself to "keep eye contact" or to "speak clearly," for example. Picture yourself actually going through the actions. Finally, imagine yourself feeling good about having been assertive. Notice how good it feels to have told someone what you wanted to say. Think how frustrated you would have felt if you had not expressed yourself. Or think how much more negatively others would have reacted if you had blown your top. Practice until you can go through it smoothly in your imagination. Then try it out in actual situations.

You could even keep track of your progress in an assertiveness diary. When you try new assertive behaviors, write down what you did, how it worked, and how you felt. It's a good way to remind yourself how you're doing.

MINDING YOUR BALANCE

How do you decide how much to pursue or continue a particular relationship? You are probably most drawn to those that offer a favorable ratio of pleasant to unpleasant interactions. Both common sense and research indicate that high-quality relationships are those with people who are trustworthy and supportive, with many more positive than negative interactions.[3] Having more positive and fewer negative relationships predicts both physical and mental health.[3,4]

One straightforward way to maintain relationships, then, is to offer many more positive than negative interactions. Having at least five times more positive than negative exchanges has been called a "magic" ratio for teachers,[5,6] but trying to keep count may drive you crazy. The point is to increase genuine positive communications (appreciation, warmth, compliments, and such) and minimize negative ones (e.g., criticism, blame, or contempt) that can have disproportionate impact, souring a host of positives.

In close relationships over time, it's easy to let your ratio slip, forgetting or neglecting to be kind ("taking for granted"). Positive exchanges are like making a deposit in the savings account of your relationship, and negative exchanges are like withdrawals. Furthermore, within the context of an overall positive relationship, negatives can particularly sting. You are responsible to be kind to those whom you have "tamed."[7]

EXPRESSING POSITIVE AND NEGATIVE FEELINGS

When you express negative feelings, concentrate on being polite but clear. If you're uncomfortable with what someone is doing, it's usually okay to let them know. This does not mean that you need to insult, shame, or intimidate. If you do so, the person is likely to become defensive, making it harder for you to communicate clearly. A good test is to imagine how you would prefer to be told something negative, so that you could hear and understand the person's feelings without feeling threatened or humiliated. Then try it.

It's also okay, under most circumstances, to let people know your positive feelings. If you like what someone has done, for example, you can say so without hesitation. You have every right to do so, and most people enjoy hearing compliments even if they become a bit self-conscious. Again, try to imagine how you would like a person to tell you something positive, then try doing it that way.

SO, WHAT DO YOU SAY?

Some people find they get stuck in deciding exactly what words to use. There are many different ways of saying the same thing effectively. The precise words are not as important as getting the message across clearly. Nevertheless, you do need words, and it's a good idea to think through how you might say something in an assertive manner. Here are some examples of assertive statements:

"Please don't smoke. It really bothers me."

"I feel great being here with you."

"I feel annoyed when you're late, and this is the third time."

"No, thanks. I've eaten enough, and any more would spoil it."

"I need a hand with this. Can you help me, please?"

"You handled that beautifully."

"I really don't have time to help you until next week."

"I don't like being called 'Honey'!"

"That movie doesn't interest me."

"Sunday is a bad night for me, but how about Friday or Saturday instead?"

"I really appreciate it when you tell me what you like."

"I want to talk to you about something that's been on my mind."

"Excuse me. I was here first."

"Please give me another package. This one has been opened."

ASSERTIVENESS IN ACTION

To help you think about situations in which assertiveness can be useful, here are a few examples.

• You're visiting relatives, and your uncle Bob begins his usual inquiry about when you're going to get "a decent job." You're tired of having to justify yourself to him and the rest of your family, and you know that if the conversation continues you'll become angry.

Bob: So when are you going to settle into a decent job? Any prospects yet?

You: Uncle Bob, I know you care about me, but I'd really rather you didn't ask me about my job every time we talk. Let's discuss something else and enjoy being together, okay?

• You are single and have just gone out with someone for the first time. You really enjoyed yourself but find it hard to say so. In this case, telling the person how good you feel would be an assertive act. It need not be a magnificent statement. It need only convey the message "I enjoyed being with you." You could use these words or be more specific about what you did enjoy:

> "I really enjoyed dancing with you tonight."
>
> "This was a relaxing afternoon. You're fun to be with."
>
> "You're an interesting person to spend time with."
>
> "I appreciate talking to someone who is as interested in music as I am."

• Your best friend is pushing drinks on someone you know is trying to cut down. You're annoyed at your friend and think she isn't being fair. An assertive response here might involve taking your friend aside and saying, "Hey, I wonder if you realize that Sam wants to cut down on his drinking. It's hard for him, and it's even harder when people push drinks on him. How about helping him out?"

• A salesperson calls you on the phone and asks for a few minutes of your time. You could afford the time but really don't want to buy anything. Besides, you dislike sales talk. The salesperson says, "Just let me describe our offer, no obligation. If you don't find our offer beneficial, you haven't lost anything." One assertive response would be "No, thank you. I'm not interested. Goodbye," and hang up.

CONFLICTS IN CLOSE RELATIONSHIPS

Relationship conflicts can interact with alcohol in at least two ways. First of all, having conflict in a close relationship can lead to drinking, with alcohol used for escape, forgetting, or even revenge.[8] Second, drinking can precede and contribute to conflict.[9] In other words, drinking can both affect and be affected by conflict in relationships.[10] Having skills for peacefully resolving conflict can help you maintain important relationships.

Living in harmony with others requires a continual give and take—a kind of compromising. Often this happens naturally, without much awareness. At times, however, one or another person becomes dissatisfied with the result of this natural process and conflict arises.

Often people are able to come up with an acceptable solution to a problem by talking it over and arriving at a common understanding. This requires attention to each other's needs and wants. If just talking it over does not produce the needed changes, then some negotiation may yield a solution.

By *negotiation* we mean a method for resolving problems between people who are important to each other. It is a way for people to respect and understand each other while arranging for their own needs to be met. Here is a brief outline of how the process can work.

1. When a conflict arises in a relationship, set a time to discuss it. Put aside a period that is reserved solely for solving the problem. Negotiation deserves your full attention. Arrange a time and place where you won't be interrupted. Once you've agreed on when to discuss it, don't waste time rehashing the conflict before your negotiation session.

2. Commit yourself to seeking a constructive and mutually satisfying "win–win" solution to the problem. Think of the problem as something that is neither inside you nor inside the other person but is in your *relationship*—it affects you both. Avoid unfair and provocative actions, such as blaming, insulting, threatening, or bringing up old complaints. Stay focused on the *problem* you've agreed to discuss, not on who is to blame. Talk over just one conflict at a time.

3. Begin by getting a clear picture of the conflict. Each person could write down the *specific actions they see* as being the problem. For example:

- "You haven't paid the bills on time as we agreed you would."
- "You tie up the bathroom for half an hour in the morning."

This can be difficult. Be careful to avoid general name-calling complaints that only sound like the problem:

- Too general: "You're inconsiderate."
- Better: "Please call when you're going to be late."
- Too general: "You're sloppy."
- Better: "I feel irritated when you leave your work on the kitchen table."

Note that statements beginning with "You" sound very accusatory. Statements that focus on what you feel or prefer are less troubling.

4. Clearly specify what changes you would like. If you have carefully specified the problem in Step 3, this is much easier. For example:

- "If you'll put the mail here on the desk, I'll check for bills every day and make sure they're paid on time."
- "I will spend no more than 20 minutes in the bathroom in the morning."

Negotiations tend to have a more balanced feeling if each partner ends up with one change to make. Remember that it is essential that the change be specified clearly. It should be obvious to a neutral observer when the change has been made and when it has not.

5. When the other person makes a change in behavior as requested, be sure to notice and comment positively on it. Consider doing something nice as a "thank you."

Consider seeking outside assistance if you cannot reach

mutually satisfying solutions, if you cannot negotiate without becoming embroiled in an argument, or if conflicts escalate toward physical violence. A neutral third perspective can be helpful, and many psychologists, counselors, and other helping professionals have special training and experience in resolving relationship problems.

RESOURCES

Relationships

- The research-based Our Relationship program to strengthen intimate relationships can be found online (*www.ourrelationship.com*) or through the app stores. As an affordable alternative to couple therapy, it takes 4–6 weeks to complete in self-directed or coach-guided form.
- John Gottman and colleagues at the University of Washington have done decades of outstanding research on what actually helps intimate relationships last: Gottman, J. M., & DeClaire, J. (2017). *The relationship cure: A 5 step guide to strengthening your marriage, family, and friendships.* Harmony. Many other resources are available at *www.gottman.com*
- Christensen, A., Doss, B. D., & Jacobson, N. S. (2014). *Reconcilable differences: Rebuild your relationship by rediscovering the partner you love—without losing yourself* (2nd ed.). Guilford Press.

Assertiveness

- There are abundant books, videos, courses, and free resources to be found by searching the term *assertiveness* in a browser. Here's a quick summary from the Mayo Clinic: *www.mayoclinic.org/healthy-lifestyle/stress-management/in-depth/assertive/art-20044644*
- In books, a time-tested option that is currently in its 10th edition is *Your Perfect Right: Assertiveness and Equality in Your Life and Relationships* by Robert Alberti and Michael Emmons. Another best-seller is Judy Murphy's *Assertiveness: How to Stand Up for Yourself and Still Win the Respect of Others.*

22

MOVING ALONG

At this point you have been thoroughly rethinking drinking. You've considered the pros and cons of drinking, completed a personal checkup, perhaps tried some steps to change your own use of alcohol, and explored some alternatives to drinking to help you get what you want out of life.

So, what are you now thinking that you'll do? You don't need to have "a problem" with drinking to decide what to do going forward. How important is alcohol for you, and why? Perhaps you've already been trying some of the methods in Part Three to reduce your use of alcohol. If so, how is it going? What would be some of the pros and cons of trying out being a nondrinker, at least for a while? The choice is always yours.

PERSONAL FREEDOM OR CLAUSTROPHOBIA?

Some people choose to keep on drinking just to show that they can. A decision to cut down on or refrain from alcohol sometimes takes on extra meaning. It may feel like:

- Being restricted or deprived
- Admitting that you have "a problem"
- Having to grow up
- Having someone "holier than thou" telling you what to do
- Saying goodbye to all fun and enjoyment in life

Such thoughts can create a feeling of mental imprisonment, and people naturally resist restriction of freedom. If there are other people who *want* you not to drink, that can also get in the way—"I'll be damned if I'm going to do that just because they want me to"—even if part of you actually wants to do what they're suggesting. All of these are the result of how you *think* about alcohol. If drinking is equated with your personal worth, freedom, youth, success, or happiness, then of course you wouldn't want to minimize or give it up. But you can simply decide that your life would be better with this change. In this way, decreasing or desisting alcohol use can mean *more* rather than less freedom.

What is important first and foremost is to have a rewarding life that does not depend on alcohol. Only then is drinking alcohol really a choice. When you're not enjoying life, the real or imagined pleasures of drugs can seem more enticing. Remember that over half of adults are already occasional or nondrinkers, so obviously it's possible to live without alcohol. Whatever you decide to do, find and embrace pleasures, meaning, relationships, and happiness in life without relying on alcohol.

IF YOU DECIDE TO TRY DRINKING MODERATELY

For 50 years we've been offering practical, evidence-based recommendations for people who want to drink moderately.[1] At first, we wrote primarily for heavier drinkers seeking to reduce their use, but the science is equally useful for people deciding whether and how much to drink.

If alcohol has not caused you harm or problems, just make a conscious choice about drinking (Chapter 7) and stick to it. The chapters of Part Four may also help you navigate life challenges without relying on alcohol.

If you want to *reduce* your alcohol use, how long does that take? In our studies most people who succeeded in moderating their drinking with these methods made substantial reductions within about 6 weeks. On average, they cut their drinking at least in half during this time. People working with our approach continued to reduce their drinking over a period of 3 months, after which their average drinking did not either decrease or increase much.[2–5] So you should be seeing good progress within 6 to 8 weeks. Our experience with this approach shows that if you haven't managed a good reduction in your drinking within 10 to 12 weeks, it's unlikely to happen later, unless you try something else. One option is to try abstaining completely. Professional help is also a possibility.

Please know that if you're making good progress but experiencing some setbacks, you're not alone. If you do happen to overdrink and exceed your goals, get right back on track the next day. There is no point in beating up on yourself about it. Most people who have successfully moderated their drinking have still had occasional days of excess.

As a caution: It can happen that, as people decrease their use of alcohol, they compensate with increased use of another drug. That is, you substitute one drug for another. By "drug" we mean to include tobacco, marijuana, prescription medicines (such as tranquilizers and sedatives), and over-the-counter medicines (such as sleeping aids and aspirin), as well as consciousness-altering legal and illicit drugs. If you use any of these substances, be mindful of the extent to which you are using them as you work on reducing your drinking. Be alert to this possibility. However, we found that most people do not, in fact, create another problem when they cut down on drinking; to the contrary, other aspects of their lives get better.[6]

IF YOU DECIDE TO TRY NOT DRINKING

If you already drink moderately or have been able to cut down your drinking significantly by using Part Three of this book, it should be easier to continue reducing it to zero. In other words, if you have been able to have just one or two drinks per day, then it's likely possible for you to "cut down" to no drinks per day with minimal discomfort. It can help to limit your exposure to alcohol in preparation for this change. For example, dispose of all alcoholic beverages at home and avoid being around people who are drinking for some period of time. This can be helpful until you feel comfortable abstaining even when exposed to alcohol and when around others who drink.

If you plan to quit and are still drinking large amounts daily, it may be wise to seek professional support. Effective science-based treatment methods are available to help people quit substance use.[7] In addition, if you're still drinking heavily, it's important to ensure that you have the medical help you need if you happen to encounter significant withdrawal symptoms.

In any case, the material in Part Four may be helpful in establishing an alcohol-free lifestyle. The same set of abilities (to shape your day-to-day life, to change yourself, to maintain a healthy level of pleasant activities, to sleep well, to relax, to manage anxiety and depression, and so on) can therefore be useful whether your goal is moderation or abstinence. After all, the idea is that you can do these things without needing to use alcohol.

Giving up any habit can be challenging, though most people who stop drinking or smoking do so on their own. You are more likely to succeed if you:

- Have already cut down your alcohol use
- Have friends or relatives who support and encourage you
- Have personal resources that provide a sense of balance, such as a physical exercise routine, spiritual practices, community service commitments, hobbies, or other recreational pursuits
- Have a fairly stable lifestyle, including a steady daily routine, meaningful work, regular contacts with other people, and goals toward which you are working
- Have previously been able to make significant positive changes in your life

If these descriptions do not fit you, it may be more challenging to stop drinking on your own, and we recommend that you consider obtaining professional consultation or joining a mutual support group such as Alcoholics Anonymous (*www.aa.org*), Smart Recovery (*www.smartrecovery.org*), or Women for Sobriety (*www.womenforsobriety.org*).

POSTSCRIPT

One reason we two have continued working in this field for so long is that most people *do* succeed in making changes that improve their lives. Yes, alcohol, like tobacco, is a dangerous drug with the potential to cause serious harm and ensnare people in compulsive use. But it has also been around for a very long time, and many people have learned to use it without causing problems for themselves or others. Recent information about risks to health in even moderate amounts has led many to rethink drinking. Making your own rational choice about drinking is far preferable to waiting for some major life event to occur that forces you to change. It may even prevent such an event from ever happening. We wish you all the best in choosing your own way.

NOTES

CHAPTER 1. THE PUZZLE OF ALCOHOL

1. Saad, L. (2025, August 13). *U.S. drinking rate at new low as alcohol concerns surge.* Gallup Organization.
2. Warrington, R. (2019). *Sober curious: The blissful sleep, greater focus, limitless presence, and deep connection awaiting us all on the other side of alcohol.* HarperOne.
3. Murthy, V. H. (2023). *Our epidemic of loneliness and isolation: The U.S. Surgeon General's advisory on the healing effects of social connection and community.* U.S. Department of Health and Human Services.
4. Wilkinson, R., & Pickett, K. (2009). *The spirit level: Why greater equality makes societies stronger.* Bloomsbury Press.
5. Pikety, T. (2022). *A brief history of equality* (S. Rendall, Trans.). Belknap Press.
6. Office of the Surgeon General. (2025). *Alcohol and cancer risk: The U.S. Surgeon General's advisory.* U.S. Department of Health and Human Services.
7. Kerr, W. C., Greenfield, T. K., & Tujague, J. (2006). Estimates of the mean alcohol concentration of the spirits, wine, and beer sold in the United States and per capita consumption: 1950 to 2002. *Alcoholism: Clinical and Experimental Research, 30*(9), 1583–1591.
8. Miller, W. R., & Muñoz, R. F. (1976). *How to control your drinking.* Prentice-Hall.

9. Greenfield, T. K., & Rogers, J. D. (1999). Who drinks most of the alcohol in the US? The policy implications. *Journal of Studies on Alcohol, 60*(1), 78–89.
10. American Psychiatric Association. (1980). *Diagnostic and statistical manual of mental disorders* (3rd ed.). Author.
11. American Psychiatric Association. (2013). *Diagnostic and statistical manual of mental disorders* (5th ed.). Author.
12. Fell, J. C., & Voas, R. B. (2006). The effectiveness of reducing illegal blood alcohol concentration (BAC) limits for driving: Evidence for lowering the limit to .05 BAC. *Journal of Safety Research, 37*(3), 233–243.
13. Moskowitz, H., & Florentino, D. (2000). *A review of the literature on the effects of low doses of alcohol on driving-related skills* (DOT HS 809 028). U.S. Department of Transportation, National Highway Traffic Safety Administration.
14. Bohn, M. K., Liu, Y., Esser, M. B., Mesnick, J. B., Lu, H., Pan, Y., & Greenlund, K. J. (2021, October 15). Binge drinking among adults, by select characteristics and state—United States, 2018. *Morbidity and Mortality Weekly Report, 70*(41), 1441–1446.
15. Hasin, D. S., Stinson, F. S., Ogburn, E., & Grant, B. F. (2007). Prevalence, correlates, disability, and comorbidity of DSM-IV alcohol abuse and dependence in the United States: Results from the National Epidemiologic Survey on Alcohol and Related Conditions. *Archives of General Psychiatry, 64*(7), 830–842.
16. Cahalan, D. (1970). *Problem drinkers.* Jossey-Bass.
17. American Psychiatric Association. (1994). *Diagnostic and statistical manual of mental disorders* (4th ed.). Author.
18. Bondy, S. J., Rehm, J., Ashley, M. J., Walsh, G., Single, E., & Room, R. (1999). Low-risk drinking guidelines: The scientific evidence. *Canadian Journal of Public Health, 90*(4), 264–270.
19. Phillips, J. A. (2021). Dietary guidelines for Americans, 2020–2025. *Workplace Health and Safety, 69*(8), 395.
20. World Health Organization. (2024). Alcohol. Retrieved April 22, 2025, from *www.who.int/news-room/fact-sheets/detail/alcohol*

CHAPTER 2. REASONS FOR DRINKING

1. Saad, L. (2025, August 13). *U.S. drinking rate at new low as alcohol concerns surge.* Gallup Organization.
2. Task Force on the Social and Health Effects of Alcohol Use and Abuse.

(1986). *Alcohol use and abuse: The social and health effects.* The Presbyterian Church (U.S.A.).
3. I Timothy 5:23.
4. Naimi, T. S., Brown, D. W., Brewer, R. D., Giles, W. H., Mensah, G., Serdula, M. K., . . . Stroup, D. F. (2005). Cardiovascular risk factors and confounders among nondrinking and moderate-drinking US adults. *American Journal of Preventive Medicine, 28*(4), 369–373.
5. Zhao, J., Stockwell, T., Naimi, T., Churchill, S., Clay, J., & Sherk, A. (2023). Association between daily alcohol intake and risk of all-cause mortality: A systematic review and meta-analyses. *JAMA Network Open, 6*(3), e236185–e236185.
6. Stockwell, T., Zhao, J., & Naimi, T. (2024). Apologizing for the alcohol industry? A comment on ISFAR's defense of alcohol's purported health benefits. *Journal of Studies on Alcohol and Drugs, 85*(1), 133–135.
7. Janis, I. L., & Mann, L. (1977). *Decision making: A psychological analysis of conflict, choice and commitment.* Free Press.
8. Schumann, A., Meyer, C., Rumpf, H.-J., Hannöver, W., Hapke, U., & John, U. (2005). Stage of change transitions and processes of change, decisional balance, and self-efficacy in smokers: A transtheoretical model validation using longitudinal data. *Psychology of Addictive Behaviors, 19*(1), 3–9.

CHAPTER 3. REASONS FOR NOT DRINKING

1. Bernards, S., Graham, K., Kuendig, H., Hettige, S., & Obot, I. (2009). "I have no interest in drinking": A cross-national comparison of reasons why men and women abstain from alcohol use. *Addiction, 104*(10), 1658–1668.
2. Rosansky, J. A., & Rosenberg, H. (2020). A systematic review of reasons for abstinence from alcohol reported by lifelong abstainers, current abstainers and former problem-drinkers. *Drug and Alcohol Review, 39*(7), 960–974.
3. Cunningham, J. A., Blomqvist, J., Koski-Jännes, A., Cordingley, J., & Callaghan, R. (2004). Characteristics of former heavy drinkers: Results from a natural history of drinking general population survey. *Contemporary Drug Problems, 31*(2), 357–369.
4. Slicker, E. K. (1997). University students' reasons for not drinking: Relationship to alcohol consumption level. *Journal of Alcohol and Drug Education, 42*(2), 83–102.

5. Huang, J.-H., DeJong, W., Schneider, S. K., & Towvim, L. G. (2011). Endorsed reasons for not drinking alcohol: A comparison of college student drinkers and abstainers. *Journal of Behavioral Medicine, 34*(1), 64–73.
6. Huss, M. (1907). *Om dryckenskapen och dess följder för den enskilde, för familjen, för kommunen, för staten* [On drunkenness and its consequences for the individual, for the family, for the community, for the nation]. Norstedt & Söners Förlag.
7. Rehm, J., Baliunas, D., Borges, G. L.,Graham, K., Irving, H., Kehoe, T., . . . Taylor, B. (2010). The relation between different dimensions of alcohol consumption and burden of disease: An overview. *Addiction, 105*(5), 817–843.
8. Osna, N. A., Donohue, T. M., Jr., & Kharbanda, K. K. (2017). Alcoholic liver disease: Pathogenesis and current management. *Alcohol Research: Current Reviews, 38*(2), 147–161.
9. Rehm, J., Samokhvalov, A. V., & Shield, K. D. (2013). Global burden of alcoholic liver diseases. *Journal of Hepatology, 59*(1), 160–168.
10. Oscar-Berman, M., & Marinković, K. (2007). Alcohol: Effects on neurobehavioral functions and the brain. *Neuropsychology Review, 17*(3), 239–257.
11. Miller, W. R., & Saucedo, C. F. (1983). Assessment of neuropsychological impairment and brain damage in problem drinkers. In C. J. Golden, J. A. Moses, Jr., J. A. Coffman, W. R. Miller, & F. D. Strider (Eds.), *Clinical neuropsychology: Interface with neurologic and psychiatric disorders* (pp. 141–195). Grune & Stratton.
12. Bühler, M., & Mann, K. (2011). Alcohol and the human brain: A systematic review of different neuroimaging methods. *Alcoholism: Clinical and Experimental Research, 35*(10), 1771–1793.
13. Guerri, C., & Pascual, M. (2010). Mechanisms involved in the neurotoxic, cognitive, and neurobehavioral effects of alcohol consumption during adolescence. *Alcohol, 44*(1), 15–26.
14. Esser, M. B., Sherk, A., Liu, Y., & Naimi, T. S. (2024, February 29). Deaths from excessive alcohol use—United States, 2016–2021. *Morbidity and Mortality Weekly Report, 73*(8), 154–161.
15. Stahre, M., Roeber, J., Kanny, D., Brewer, R. D., & Zhang, X. (2014). Contribution of excessive alcohol consumption to deaths and years of potential life lost in the United States. *Preventing Chronic Disease, 11,* E109.
16. Shield, K., Keyes, K. M., Martinez, P., Milam, A. J., Naimi, T. S., &

Rehm, J. (2025). *Draft report: Scientific findings of the alcohol intake and health study for public comment.*

17. Office of the Surgeon General. (2016, November). *Facing addiction in America: The Surgeon General's report on alcohol, drugs, and health.* U.S. Department of Health and Human Services.
18. Bujanda, L. (2000). The effects of alcohol consumption upon the gastrointestinal tract. *Journal of the American College of Gastroenterology, 95*(12), 3374–3382.
19. Federico, A., Cotticelli, G., Festi, D., Schiumerini, R., Addolorato, G., Ferrulli, A, . . . Loguercio, C. (2015). The effects of alcohol on gastrointestinal tract, liver and pancreas: Evidence-based suggestions for clinical management. *European Review for Medical and Pharmacological Sciences, 19*(10), 1922–1940.
20. Taylor, B., & Rehm, J. (2006). Moderate alcohol consumption and diseases of the gastrointestinal system: A review of pathophysiological processes. *Digestive Diseases, 23*(3-4), 177–180.
21. Irving, H. M., Samokhvalov, A. V., & Rehm, J. (2009). Alcohol as a risk factor for pancreatitis: A systematic review and meta-analysis. *Journal of the Pancreas, 10*(4), 387–392.
22. Griswold, M. G., Fullman, N., Hawley, C., Arian, N., Zimsen, S. R. M., Tymeson, H. D., . . . Gakidou, E. (2018). Alcohol use and burden for 195 countries and territories, 1990–2016: A systematic analysis for the Global Burden of Disease Study 2016. *Lancet, 392*(10152), 1015–1035.
23. Ebrahim, I. O., Shapiro, C. M., Williams, A. J., & Fenwick, P. B. (2013). Alcohol and sleep: I. Effects on normal sleep. *Alcoholism: Clinical and Experimental Research, 37*(4), 539–549.
24. Thakkar, M. M., Sharma, R., & Sahota, P. (2015). Alcohol disrupts sleep homeostasis. *Alcohol, 49*(4), 299–310.
25. He, S., Hasler, B. P., & Chakravorty, S. (2019). Alcohol and sleep-related problems. *Current Opinion in Psychology, 30,* 117–122.
26. Wannamethee, S. G., & Shaper, A. G. (2003). Alcohol, body weight, and weight gain in middle-aged men. *American Journal of Clinical Nutrition, 77*(5), 1312–1317.
27. Suter, P. M., & Tremblay, A. (2005). Is alcohol consumption a risk factor for weight gain and obesity? *Critical Reviews in Clinical Laboratory Sciences, 42*(3), 197–227.
28. Boden, J. M., & Fergusson, D. M. (2011). Alcohol and depression. *Addiction, 106*(5), 906–914.

29. Churchill, S. A., & Farrell, L. (2017). Alcohol and depression: Evidence from the 2014 health survey for England. *Drug and Alcohol Dependence, 180,* 86–92.
30. Quigley, B. M., & Leonard, K. E. (2004). Alcohol use and violence among young adults. *Alcohol Research and Health, 28*(4), 191–194.
31. Bushman, B. J., & Cooper, H. M. (1990). Effects of alcohol on human aggression: An integrative research review. *Psychological Bulletin, 107*(3), 341–354.
32. Lorenz, K., & Ullman, S. E. (2016). Alcohol and sexual assault victimization: Research findings and future directions. *Aggression and Violent Behavior, 31,* 82–94.
33. Ullman, S. E., Karabatsos, G., & Koss, M. P. (1999). Alcohol and sexual assault in a national sample of college women. *Journal of Interpersonal Violence, 14*(6), 603–625.
34. Ramstedt, M. (2001). Alcohol and suicide in 14 European countries. *Addiction, 96*(Suppl. 1), 59–75.
35. Sher, L. (2006). Alcohol consumption and suicide. *QJM, 99*(1), 57–61.

CHAPTER 4. THE EFFECTS OF ALCOHOL WHEN DRINKING

1. Christiansen, P., Townsend, G., Knibb, G., & Field, M. (2017). Bibi ergo sum: The effects of a placebo and contextual alcohol cues on motivation to drink alcohol. *Psychopharmacology (Berl.), 234*(5), 827–835.
2. Hull, J. G., & Bond, C. F. (1986). Social and behavioral consequences of alcohol consumption and expectancy: A meta-analysis. *Psychological Bulletin, 99*(3), 347–360.
3. Kirsch, D., Le, V., Kosted, R., Fromme, K., & Lippard, E. T. C. (2023). Neural underpinnings of expecting alcohol: Placebo alcohol administration alters nucleus accumbens resting state functional connectivity. *Behavioural Brain Research, 437,* 114148.
4. Bernstein, M. H., Wood, M. D., & Colby, S. M. (2016). A new paradigm for credibly administering placebo alcohol to underage drinkers. *Addictive Behaviors, 52,* 22–27.
5. Martin, C. S., Earleywine, M., Musty, R. E., Perrine, M., & Swift, R. M. (1993). Development and validation of the biphasic alcohol effects scale. *Alcoholism: Clinical and Experimental Research, 17*(1), 140–146.
6. King, A. C., De Wit, H., McNamara, P. J., & Cao, D. (2011). Rewarding,

stimulant, and sedative alcohol responses and relationship to future binge drinking. *Archives of General Psychiatry, 68*(4), 389–399.

CHAPTER 5. A PERSONAL CHECKUP

1. Miller, W. R., Sovereign, R. G., & Krege, B. (1988). Motivational interviewing with problem drinkers: II. The Drinker's Check-up as a preventive intervention. *Behavioural Psychotherapy, 16,* 251–268.
2. Miller, W. R., Benefield, R. G., & Tonigan, J. S. (1993). Enhancing motivation for change in problem drinking: A controlled comparison of two therapist styles. *Journal of Consulting and Clinical Psychology, 61,* 455–461.
3. Miller, W. R., Zweben, A., DiClemente, C., & Rychtarik, R. (1992). *Motivational enhancement therapy manual: A clinical research guide for therapists treating individuals with alcohol abuse and dependence* (Vol. 2). National Institute on Alcohol Abuse and Alcoholism.
4. Project MATCH Research Group. (1997). Matching alcoholism treatments to client heterogeneity: Project MATCH posttreatment drinking outcomes. *Journal of Studies on Alcohol, 58*(1), 7–29.
5. Hester, R. K., Squires, D. D., & Delaney, H. D. (2005). The Drinker's Check-up: 12-month outcomes of a controlled clinical trial of a standalone software program for problem drinkers. *Journal of Substance Abuse Treatment, 28,* 159–169.
6. Walters, S. T., Miller, J. E., & Chiauzzi, E. (2005). Wired for wellness: E-interventions for addressing college drinking. *Journal of Substance Abuse Treatment, 29,* 139–145.
7. Walker, D. D., Stephens, R., Roffman, R., DeMarce, J., Lozano, B., Towe, S., & Berg, B. (2011). Randomized controlled trial of motivational enhancement therapy with non-treatment-seeking adolescent cannabis users: A further test of the teen marijuana check-up. *Psychology of Addictive Behaviors, 25*(3), 474–484.
8. World Health Organization. (2024). Alcohol. *www.who.int/news-room/fact-sheets/detail/alcohol*
9. Paradis, C., Butt, P., Shield, K., Poole, N., Wells, S., Naimi, T., . . . Low-Risk Alcohol Drinking Guidelines Scientific Expert Panels. (2023). *Canada's guidance on alcohol and health: Final report.* Canadian Centre on Substance Use and Addiction.
10. Lin, L. A., Bonar, E. E., Zhang, L., Girard, R., & Coughlin, L. N.

(2022). Alcohol-involved overdose deaths in US veterans. *Drug and Alcohol Dependence, 230,* 109196.

11. White, A. M., Hingson, R. W., Pan, I.-J., & Yi, H.-Y. (2011). Hospitalizations for alcohol and drug overdoses in young adults ages 18–24 in the United States, 1999–2008: Results from the Nationwide Inpatient Sample. *Journal of Studies on Alcohol and Drugs, 72*(5), 774–786.
12. Demoura, M. C., Correia, J. P., & Madeira, F. (1967). Clinical alcohol hypoglycemia. *Annals of Internal Medicine, 66*(5), 893–905.
13. Richardson, T., Weiss, M., Thomas, P., & Kerr, D. (2005). Day after the night before: Influence of evening alcohol on risk of hypoglycemia in patients with type 1 diabetes. *Diabetes Care, 28*(7), 1801–1802.
14. Carey, M. G., Al-Zaiti, S. S., Kozik, T. M., & Pelter, M. (2014). Holiday heart syndrome. *American Journal of Critical Care, 23*(2), 171–172.
15. Syed, A., Seadler, B. D., & Joyce, D. L. (2023). Enjoy the holiday spirit, not the holiday heart. *Journal of Thoracic and Cardiovascular Surgery, 166*(6), e510–e511.
16. Ross, H. L. (1994). *Confronting drunk driving: Social policy for saving lives.* Yale University Press.
17. Compton, J. V., & Vogler, R. E. (1975). Validation of the Alco-calculator. *Psychological Reports, 36*(3), 977–978.
18. Greenberg, L. (1972). *Alco-calculator: An educational instrument.* Rutgers Center of Alcohol Studies.
19. Miller, W. R., Tonigan, J. S., & Longabaugh, R. (1995). *The Drinker Inventory of Consequences (DrInC): An instrument for assessing adverse consequences of alcohol abuse.* National Institute on Alcohol Abuse and Alcoholism.
20. Forcehimes, A. A., Tonigan, J. S., Miller, W. R., Kenna, G. A., & Baer, J. S. (2007). Psychometrics of the Drinker Inventory of Consequences (DrInC). *Addictive Behaviors, 32,* 1699–1704.
21. Hester, R. K., & Squires, D. D. (2008). Web-based norms for the Drinker Inventory of Consequences from the Drinker's Checkup. *Journal of Substance Abuse Treatment, 35*(3), 322–327.
22. Miller, W. R., Baca, C., Compton, W. M., Ernst, D., Manuel, J. K., Pringle, B., . . . Zweben, A. (2006). Addressing substance abuse in health care settings. *Alcoholism, Clinical and Experimental Research, 30*(2), 292–302.
23. Weisner, C., Mertens, J., Parthasarathy, S., Moore, C., & Lu, Y. (2001). Integrating primary medical care with addiction treatment: A randomized controlled trial. *Journal of the American Medical Association, 286,* 1715–1723.

24. Hesselbrock, V. M., O'Brien, J., Weinstein, M., & Carter-Menendez, N. (1987). Reasons for drinking and alcohol use in young adults at high risk and at low risk for alcoholism. *British Journal of Addiction, 82*(12), 1335–1339.
25. Carpenter, K. M., & Hasin, D. S. (1999). Drinking to cope with negative affect and DSM-IV alcohol use disorders: A test of three alternative explanations. *Journal of Studies on Alcohol, 60*(5), 694–704.
26. Carpenter, K. M., & Hasin, D. S. (1998). Reasons for drinking alcohol: Relationships with DSM-IV alcohol diagnoses and alcohol consumption in a community sample. *Psychology of Addictive Behaviors, 12*(3), 168–184.
27. Farber, P. D., Khavari, K. A., & Douglass, F. M. (1980). A factor analytic study of reasons for drinking: Empirical validation of positive and negative reinforcement dimensions. *Journal of Consulting and Clinical Psychology, 48*(6), 780–781.
28. Cutter, H. S., & O'Farrell, T. J. (1984). Relationship between reasons for drinking and customary drinking behavior. *Journal of Studies on Alcohol, 45*(4), 321–325.
29. Lo, C. C., & Bissler, D. L. (1998). Gender differences in reasons for drinking and not drinking: Association with drinking levels and alcohol-related consequences. *Free Inquiry in Creative Sociology, 26*(2), 135–144.
30. Zywiak, W. H., Westerberg, V. S., Connors, G. J., & Maisto, S. A. (2003). Exploratory findings from the Reasons for Drinking Questionnaire. *Journal of Substance Abuse Treatment, 25*(4), 287–292.
31. Adams, Z. W., Schacht, J. P., Randall, P., & Anton, R. F. (2016). The Reasons for Heavy Drinking Questionnaire: Factor structure and validity in alcohol-dependent adults involved in clinical trials. *Journal of Studies on Alcohol and Drugs, 77*(2), 354–361.
32. Westerberg, V. S., Miller, W. R., & Heather, N. (1996). Reasons for Drinking Questionnaire. *Addiction, 91,* S129–S130.
33. Miller, W. R., & Pechacek, T. F. (1987). New roads: Assessing and treating psychological dependence. *Journal of Substance Abuse Treatment, 4,* 73–77.

CHAPTER 6. CHOOSING YOUR OWN WAY

1. Miller, W. R., & Muñoz, R. F. (2013). *Controlling your drinking: Tools to make moderation work for you* (2nd ed.). Guilford Press.
2. Miller, W. R., Forcehimes, A. A., & Zweben, A. (2019). *Treating addiction: A guide for professionals* (2nd ed.). Guilford Press.

3. Witkiewitz, K., Maisto, S. A., & Donovan, D. M. (2010). A comparison of methods for estimating change in drinking following alcohol treatment. *Alcoholism: Clinical and Experimental Research, 34*(12), 2116–2125.
4. Janis, I. L., & Mann, L. (1977). *Decision making: A psychological analysis of conflict, choice, and commitment.* Free Press.
5. DiClemente, C. C., & Crisafulli, M. A. (2022). Relapse on the road to recovery: Learning the lessons of failure on the way to successful behavior change. *Journal of Health Service Psychology, 48,* 59–68.
6. Prochaska, J. O., Velicer, W. F., Rossi, J. S., Goldstein, M. G., Marcus, B. H., Rakowski, W., . . . Rossi, S. R. (1994). Stages of change and decisional balance for 12 problem behaviors. *Health Psychology, 13*(1), 39–46.
7. Miller, W. R., & Muñoz, R. F. (1976). *How to control your drinking.* Prentice-Hall.
8. Miller, W. R., Leckman, A. L., Delaney, H. D., & Tinkcom, M. (1992). Long-term follow-up of behavioral self-control training. *Journal of Studies on Alcohol, 53,* 249–261.
9. Miller, W. R., Gribskov, C. J., & Mortell, R. L. (1981). Effectiveness of a self-control manual for problem drinkers with and without therapist contact. *International Journal of the Addictions, 16,* 1247–1254.
10. Miller, W. R., & Taylor, C. A. (1980). Relative effectiveness of bibliotherapy, individual and group self-control training in the treatment of problem drinkers. *Addictive Behaviors, 5,* 13–24.
11. Miller, W. R., Taylor, C. A., & West, J. (1980). Focused versus broad-spectrum behavior therapy for problem drinkers. *Journal of Consulting and Clinical Psychology, 48*(5), 590–601.
12. Harris, K. B., & Miller, W. R. (1990). Behavioral self-control training for problem drinkers: Components of efficacy. *Psychology of Addictive Behaviors, 4,* 82–90.
13. Sanchez-Craig, M. (1980). Random assignment to abstinence or controlled drinking in a cognitive-behavioral program: Short-term effects on drinking behavior. *Addictive Behaviors, 5,* 35–39.
14. Vogler, R. E., Weissbach, T. A., Compton, J. V., & Martin, G. T. (1977). Integrated behavior change techniques for problem drinkers in the community. *Journal of Consulting and Clinical Psychology, 45,* 267–279.
15. Sobell, L. C., & Sobell, M. B. (2011). *Group therapy for substance use disorders: A motivational cognitive-behavioral approach.* Guilford Press.
16. Witkiewitz, K., & Marlatt, G. A. (2006). Overview of harm reduction treatments for alcohol problems. *International Journal of Drug Policy, 17*(4), 285–294.

CHAPTER 10. ON THE SPOT

1. Miller, W. R. (2022). *On second thought: How ambivalence shapes your life.* Guilford Press.

CHAPTER 12. THE HEALTHY MANAGEMENT OF REALITY

1. Muñoz, R. F., & Mendelson, T. (2005). Toward evidence-based interventions for diverse populations: The San Francisco General Hospital prevention and treatment manuals. *Journal of Consulting and Clinical Psychology, 73*(5), 790–799.
2. Muñoz, R. F., Le, H.-N., Barrera, A. Z., & Pineda, B. S. (2021). Leading the charge toward a world without depression: Perinatal depression can be prevented. *Archives of Women's Mental Health, 24*(5), 807–815.
3. Muñoz, R. F. (1996). The healthy management of reality. *https://i4health.paloaltou.edu/downloads/HMOR_English.pdf*

CHAPTER 13. KICKING BACK

1. Khir, S. M., Yunus, W. M. A. W. M., Mahmud, N., Wang, R., Panatik, S. A., Sukor, M. S. M. S., & Nordin, N. A. (2024). Efficacy of progressive muscle relaxation in adults for stress, anxiety, and depression: A systematic review. *Psychology Research and Behavior Management, 17,* 345–365.
2. Hopper, S. I., Murray, S. L., Ferrara, L. R., & Singleton, J. K. (2019). Effectiveness of diaphragmatic breathing for reducing physiological and psychological stress in adults: A quantitative systematic review. *JBI Database of Systematic Reviews and Implementation Reports, 17*(9), 1855–1876.

CHAPTER 14. HAVING FUN

1. Lewinsohn, P. M., & Graf, M. (1973). Pleasant activities and depression. *Journal of Consulting and Clinical Psychology, 41*(2), 261–268.
2. Lewinsohn, P. M., & Amenson, C. S. (1978). Some relations between pleasant and unpleasant mood-related events and depression. *Journal of Abnormal Psychology, 87*(6), 644–654.

3. Dimidjian, S., Barrera, M., Jr., Martell, C., Muñoz, R. F., & Lewinsohn, P. M. (2011). The origins and current status of behavioral activation treatments for depression. *Annual Review of Clinical Psychology, 7,* 1–38.

CHAPTER 15. AVOIDING THE BLUES

1. Muñoz, R. F., Cuijpers, P., Smit, F., Barrera, A. Z., & Leykin, Y. (2010). Prevention of major depression. *Annual Review of Clinical Psychology, 6,* 181–212.
2. Muñoz, R. F., Beardslee, W. R., & Leykin, Y. (2012). Major depression can be prevented. *American Psychologist, 67,* 285–295.
3. Muñoz, R. F., & Bunge, E. L. (2016). Prevention of depression worldwide: A wake-up call. *Lancet Psychiatry, 3*(4), 306–307.
4. Muñoz, R. F. (2019). Prevent depression in pregnancy to boost all mental health. *Nature, 574,* 631–633.
5. U.S. Preventive Services Task Force. (2019). Interventions to prevent perinatal depression: U.S. Preventive Services Task Force recommendation statement. *JAMA, 321*(6), 580–587.
6. O'Connor, E. A., Rossom, R. C., Miller, M., & Schultz, C. A. (2019). Screening for perinatal depression: A systematic evidence review for the U.S. Preventive Services Task Force. *JAMA, 321*(6), 588–601.
7. Hall, S. M., Muñoz, R. F., Reus, V. I., & Sees, K. L. (1993). Nicotine, negative affect, and depression. *Journal of Consulting and Clinical Psychology, 61*(5), 761–767.
8. Centers for Disease Control and Prevention. (2023). QuickStats: Age-adjusted percentage of adults aged ≥18 years who experienced depression in the past 12 months, by sex—National Health Interview Survey, United States, 2021–2023. National Center for Health Statistics. *www.cdc.gov/nchs/data/nhis/earlyrelease/depression-trend-2023.pdf*
9. Kuehner, C. (2017). Why is depression more common among women than among men? *Lancet Psychiatry, 4*(2), 146–158.
10. Gross, J. J., & Muñoz, R. F. (1995). Emotion regulation and mental health. *Clinical Psychology: Science and Practice, 2*(2), 151–164.
11. *www.brainyquote.com/search_results?x=0&y=0&q=On+thoughts*
12. *https://willpolston.com/the-top-10-marcus-aurelius-quotes-about-stoicism*
13. Ellis, A., & MacLaren, C. (2005). *Rational emotive behavior therapy: A therapist's guide* (2nd ed.). Impact.
14. Beck, A. T., Rush, A. J., Shaw, B. F., Emery, G., DeRubeis, R. J., &

Hollon, S. D. (2024). *Cognitive therapy of depression* (2nd ed.). Guilford Press.

CHAPTER 16. FEELING GOOD ABOUT YOURSELF

1. Yeager, D. S., Hanselman, P., Walton, G. M., Murray, J. S., Crosnoe, R., Muller, C., . . . Dweck, C. S. (2019). A national experiment reveals where a growth mindset improves achievement. *Nature, 573* (7774), 364–369.
2. Smith, S. (1850). Lecture XIX: On the conduct of the understanding (Part II). *Elementary sketches of moral philosophy. Delivered at the Royal Institution, in the years 1804, 1805, and 1806* (p. 220). Longman, Brown, Green, and Longmans.
3. Han, A., & Kim, T. H. (2023). Effects of self-compassion interventions on reducing depressive symptoms, anxiety, and stress: A meta-analysis. *Mindfulness, 14*(3), 1–29.

CHAPTER 17. GETTING THE SLEEP YOU NEED

1. Benjafield, A., Sert Kuniyoshi, F., Malhotra, A., Maurer, L., Morin, C., Martin, J., & Wickwire, E. (2024). Americas prevalence of insomnia disorder in adults: Estimation using currently available data. *Sleep, 47*(Suppl. 1), A173–A174.
2. Miller, M. B., Donahue, M. L., Carey, K. B., & Scott-Sheldon, L. A. (2017). Insomnia treatment in the context of alcohol use disorder: A systematic review and meta-analysis. *Drug and Alcohol Dependence, 181,* 200–207.
3. Qaseem, A., Kansagara, D., Forciea, M. A., Cooke, M., & Denberg, T. D. (2016). Management of chronic insomnia disorder in adults: A clinical practice guideline from the American College of Physicians. *Annals of Internal Medicine, 165*(2), 125–133.
4. Geoffroy, P. A., Lejoyeux, M., & Rolland, B. (2020). Management of insomnia in alcohol use disorder. *Expert Opinion on Pharmacotherapy, 21*(3), 297–306.
5. Zhong, C., Masters, M., Donzella, S. M., O'Connell, S., Sinner, F. C., Han, P., . . . Alcala, D. C. (2025). Electronic screen use and sleep duration and timing in adults. *JAMA Network Open, 8*(3), e252493.
6. Miller, W. R., & DiPilato, M. (1983). Treatment of nightmares via

relaxation and desensitization: A controlled evaluation. *Journal of Consulting and Clinical Psychology, 51*(6), 870–877.

7. Ritterband, L. M., Shaffer, K. M., Thorndike, F. P., Chow, P. I., Gonder-Frederick, L., Ingersoll, K. S., . . . Morin, C. M. (2025). A randomized controlled trial of a digital cognitive behavioral therapy for insomnia for older adults. *NPJ Digital Medicine, 8,* 458.

CHAPTER 18. TUNING IN INSTEAD OF OUT

1. Calderone, A., Latella, D., Impellizzeri, F., de Pasquale, P., Famà, F., Quartarone, A., & Calabrò, R. S. (2024). Neurobiological changes induced by mindfulness and meditation: A systematic review. *Biomedicines, 12*(11), 2613.
2. Dahl, C. J., Wilson-Mendenhall, C. D., & Davidson, R. J. (2020). The plasticity of well-being: A training-based framework for the cultivation of human flourishing. *Proceedings of the National Academy of Sciences, 117*(51), 32197–32206.
3. Khoury, B., Sharma, M., Rush, S. E., & Fournier, C. (2015). Mindfulness-based stress reduction for healthy individuals: A meta-analysis. *Journal of Psychosomatic Research, 78*(6), 519–528.
4. Galante, J., Friedrich, C., Collaboration of Mindfulness Trials (CoMinT), Dalgleish, T., Jones, P. B., & White, I. R. (2023). Systematic review and individual participant data meta-analysis of randomized controlled trials assessing mindfulness-based programs for mental health promotion. *Nature Mental Health, 1,* 462–476.
5. Nandarathana, N., & Ranjan, J. K. (2025). The efficacy and durability of mindfulness-based cognitive therapy in the treatment of anxiety and depressive disorders: A systematic review and meta-analysis. *Indian Journal of Psychological Medicine, 47*(3), 214–222.
6. Li, W., Howard, M. O., Garland, E. L., McGovern, P., & Lazar, M. (2017). Mindfulness treatment for substance misuse: A systematic review and meta-analysis. *Journal of Substance Abuse Treatment, 75,* 62–96.
7. Sancho, M., De Gracia, M., Rodríguez, R. C., Mallorquí-Bagué, N., Sánchez-González, J., Trujols, J., . . . Menchón, J. M. (2018). Mindfulness-based interventions for the treatment of substance and behavioral addictions: A systematic review. *Frontiers in Psychiatry, 9,* 95.
8. Kabat-Zinn, J., Lipworth, L., & Burney, R. (1985). The clinical use of

mindfulness meditation for the self-regulation of chronic pain. *Journal of Behavioral Medicine, 8*(2), 163–190.

9. Kabat-Zinn, J., Massion, A. O., Kristeller, J., Peterson, L. G., Fletcher, K. E., Pbert, L., . . . Santorelli, S. F. (1992). Effectiveness of a meditation-based stress reduction program in the treatment of anxiety disorders. *American Journal of Psychiatry, 149*(7), 936–943.
10. Kuyken, W., Warren, F. C., Taylor, R. S., Whalley, B., Crane, C., Bondolfi, G., . . . Dalgleish, T. (2016). Efficacy of mindfulness-based cognitive therapy in prevention of depressive relapse: An individual patient data meta-analysis from randomized trials. *JAMA Psychiatry, 73*(6), 565–574.

CHAPTER 19. QUIETING FEAR

1. Papola, D., Miguel, C., Mazzaglia, M., Franco, P., Tedeschi, F., Romero, S. A., . . . Barbui, C. (2024). Psychotherapies for generalized anxiety disorder in adults: A systematic review and network meta-analysis of randomized clinical trials. *JAMA Psychiatry, 81*(3), 250–259.
2. Carpenter, J. K., Andrews, L. A., Witcraft, S. M., Powers, M. B., Smits, J. A. J., & Hofmann, S. G. (2018). Cognitive behavioral therapy for anxiety and related disorders: A meta-analysis of randomized placebo-controlled trials. *Depression and Anxiety, 35*(6), 502–514.

CHAPTER 20. FORMING RELATIONSHIPS

1. Cohen, S. (2004). Social relationships and health. *American Psychologist, 59*(8), 676–684.
2. Leigh-Hunt, N., Bagguley, D., Bash, K., Turner, V., Turnbull, S., Valtorta, N., & Caan, W. (2017). An overview of systematic reviews on the public health consequences of social isolation and loneliness. *Public Health, 152,* 157–171.
3. Singer, C. (2018). Health effects of social isolation and loneliness. *Journal of Aging Life Care, 28*(1), 4–8.
4. Gordon, T. (1970). *Parent effectiveness training.* Wyden.
5. Nichols, M. P., & Straus, M. B. (2021). *The lost art of listening: How learning to listen can improve relationships* (3rd ed.). Guilford Press.
6. Miller, W. R. (2018). *Listening well: The art of empathic understanding.* Wipf & Stock.

CHAPTER 21. KEEPING RELATIONSHIPS

1. Gordon, T. (2001). *Leader Effectiveness Training: Proven skills for leading today's business into tomorrow.* Berkley.
2. Gordon, T. (1970). *Parent effectiveness training.* Wyden.
3. Ross, K. M., Rook, K., Winczewski, L., Collins, N., & Dunkel Schetter, C. (2019). Close relationships and health: The interactive effect of positive and negative aspects. *Social and Personality Psychology Compass, 13*(6), e12468.
4. Lee, H. J., & Szinovacz, M. E. (2016). Positive, negative, and ambivalent interactions with family and friends: Associations with well-being. *Journal of Marriage and Family, 78*(3), 660–679.
5. Cook, C. R., Grady, E. A., Long, A. C., Renshaw, T., Codding, R. S., Fiat, A., & Larson, M. (2017). Evaluating the impact of increasing general education teachers' ratio of positive-to-negative interactions on students' classroom behavior. *Journal of Positive Behavior Interventions, 19*(2), 67–77.
6. Sabey, C. V., Charlton, C., & Charlton, S. R. (2019). The "magic" positive-to-negative interaction ratio: Benefits, applications, cautions, and recommendations. *Journal of Emotional and Behavioral Disorders, 27*(3), 154–164.
7. Saint-Exupéry, A. de. (1943). *The little prince.* Harcourt.
8. Flanagan, J. C., Jarnecke, A. M., Leone, R. M., & Oesterle, D. W. (2020). Effects of couple conflict on alcohol craving: Does intimate partner violence play a role? *Addictive Behaviors, 109,* 106474.
9. Eckhardt, C. I., Parrott, D. J., & Crane, C. A. (2019). Alcohol, conflict, and aggression in intimate relationships: A dyadic approach. *Journal of Social and Personal Relationships, 36*(5), 1459–1475.
10. Rodriguez, L. M., Neighbors, C., & Knee, C. R. (2014). Problematic alcohol use and marital distress: An interdependence theory perspective. *Addiction Research and Theory, 22*(4), 294–312.

CHAPTER 22. MOVING ALONG

1. Miller, W. R., & Muñoz, R. F. (1976). *How to control your drinking.* Prentice-Hall.
2. Miller, W. R., Leckman, A. L., Delaney, H. D., & Tinkcom, M. (1992).

Long-term follow-up of behavioral self-control training. *Journal of Studies on Alcohol, 53,* 249–261.

3. Miller, W. R., Gribskov, C. J., & Mortell, R. L. (1981). Effectiveness of a self-control manual for problem drinkers with and without therapist contact. *International Journal of the Addictions, 16,* 1247–1254.
4. Miller, W. R., & Taylor, C. A. (1980). Relative effectiveness of bibliotherapy, individual and group self-control training in the treatment of problem drinkers. *Addictive Behaviors, 5,* 13–24.
5. Harris, K. B., & Miller, W. R. (1990). Behavioral self-control training for problem drinkers: Components of efficacy. *Psychology of Addictive Behaviors, 4,* 82–90.
6. Miller, W. R., Hedrick, K. E., & Taylor, C. A. (1983). Addictive behaviors and life problems before and after behavioral treatment of problem drinkers. *Addictive Behaviors, 8*(4), 403–412.
7. Miller, W. R., Forcehimes, A. A., & Zweben, A. (2019). *Treating addiction: A guide for professionals* (2nd ed.). Guilford Press.

INDEX

Note. *f* or *t* following a page number indicates a figure or table.

ABOUT THE AUTHORS

William R. Miller, PhD, is Emeritus Distinguished Professor of Psychology and Psychiatry at the University of New Mexico. Fundamentally interested in the psychology of change, he cofounded the counseling method of motivational interviewing and has focused in particular on developing ways to prevent and treat addiction. He is a recipient of two career achievement awards from the American Psychological Association, the international Jellinek Memorial Award, and an Innovators Award from the Robert Wood Johnson Foundation, among many other honors.

Ricardo F. Muñoz, PhD, is Professor Emeritus of Psychology at the University of California, San Francisco, and Distinguished Professor Emeritus at Palo Alto University. He was inducted as a Fellow of the American Association for the Advancement of Science in recognition of his distinguished contributions to the treatment and prevention of depression and the development of internet interventions to improve mental health worldwide.